Jonathan Neale was born in New York City and has lived in London since 1966. He has worked as a sailing teacher, anthropologist, hospital porter, carpenter, abortion counsellor and playwright. He studied social history at the University of Warwick and is the author of *Memoirs of a Callous Picket* (Pluto 1983).

# JONATHAN NEALE

# The Cutlass and the Lash

*Mutiny and Discipline in Nelson's Navy*

## PLUTO PRESS
London and Sydney

First published in 1985 by Pluto Press Limited,
The Works, 105a Torriano Avenue, London NW5 2RX
and Pluto Press Australia Limited, PO Box 199, Leichhardt,
New South Wales 2040, Australia

7 6 5 4 3 2 1

89 88 87 86 85

Diagram on page 19 by John Chesterman

Phototypeset by AKM Associates (UK) Limited,
Ajmal House, Hayes Road, Southall, London
Printed in Great Britain by Guernsey Press Co. Ltd.
Guernsey, C.I.

British Library Cataloguing in Publication Data
Neale, Jonathan
    The cutlass and lash : mutiny and discipline in Nelson's navy.
    1. Great Britain. *Royal Navy* —— Sea life
    I. Title
    359.1′0941      V737
ISBN 0 7453 0079 0

This book is for my father and mother

# Contents

# Preface

This book is about mutiny and discipline in the Royal Navy during the long war against the French from 1793 to 1815. Chapter 1 is an introduction to life on board ship. Chapter 2 is about discipline: what the Navy called 'punishment'. Chapter 3 describes the various forms of resistance the seamen found, from 'murmuring' to 'mutiny'. Chapter 4 deals with the politics and trade union traditions of the forecastle. The rest of the book focuses on two mutinies: the *Culloden* in 1794 and the *Defiance* in 1795.

*The Cutlass and the Lash* is the first fruit of my study of industrial relations in Nelson's Navy. I deal with the great mutinies of 1797 only in passing, as they will be the subject of the sequel to this book.

The University of Warwick gave me a grant which enabled me to do much of the research. I am very grateful. Parts of this book were submitted in a different form as an MA thesis 'Discipline and Mutiny in the Royal Navy, 1793–1803' (1984) to the Centre for the Study of Social History at the University of Warwick.

I owe some personal debts. My grandfather, Paul Sheldon, and my father, Walter C. Neale, taught me their love of the sea and of nautical and naval history. At Warwick, Tony Mason, Jim Obelkevich and Bruce Laurie were delightful teachers. Tony was both a demanding and an encouraging supervisor. John Molyneux and Portsmouth SWP provided great encouragement. Linda Neale has read the whole book twice and talked it over a hundred times, giving me the advice of a talented writer and a passionate historian. As always, living with her is both a privilege and an education.

# Prologue: 'I have been a republican since the beginning of the war'

HMS *Hermione* was an unhappy ship. Captain Wilkinson seemed addicted to the lash, and two men had died after repeated beatings. When Hugh Pigot replaced Captain Wilkinson, the men held their breath. Pigot turned out to be no better. He was a shouter, a bully and a flogger.[1]

In the late afternoon of 20 February 1797, the frigate ran into a sudden Caribbean squall off the coast of Puerto Rico. Captain Pigot ordered his men aloft to reef the topsails – to take in part of the highest sails so that the ship did not lean over too far in the wind. The men leapt up the rigging. The mizzenmast rose from the quarterdeck where Pigot stood, so the men on the mizzentop were directly under his eye. Captain Pigot felt they were working too slowly, and he yelled up at them that he would flog the last man down.

The men in the mizzentop believed him. Many captains did the same, especially when the admiral was watching. It was unfair. The first two men up the rigging would go out to the end of the yards, the wooden booms the men stood on to work the sails. They would therefore have to be the last two men down. But many captains felt it encouraged the others.

The Hermiones – crews were generally called after their ships – were certainly frightened. They raced back along the yards as the wind made the ship yaw back and forth. Then, at the same moment, three men fell from the mizzen yard:

1

William Johnson, a 15-year-old orphan from England; Peter Bascomb, a 16-year-old black man from Barbados; the third is not recorded. All three died as they hit the deck.

The men in the maintop were still gathering in the larger mainsail. They looked wordlessly down on the deck. Nobody seems to have moved. Captain Pigot shouted an order, 'Throw the lubbers overboard.'

The maintopmen were the most experienced and respected sailors among the crew. They began to murmer among themselves. Down on deck Pigot could not hear what they were saying, but he could guess. He ordered the boatswain's mates into the rigging to 'start' the maintopmen. The boatswain's mates went up the rigging and out along the yards, beating the maintopmen about the head and shoulders with stout ropes. The maintopmen had to hang on for dear life and could not defend themselves.

The men on deck threw the bodies overboard. Sailors were not religious men, and in the heat of battle would throw the dead over the side without a second thought. But there was no battle here, and the bodies should not have been denied divine service.

When the maintopmen came down to the deck Pigot ordered their names to be taken so they could be flogged the next day for insubordination. That night several of the crew met and decided to take the ship, but when morning came they had done nothing. Perhaps they were frightened.

At noon the maintopmen were flogged. David Casey, a midshipman on the *Hermione* that day, was later to record that '*A very severe punishment* of several men, I believe twelve or fourteen, took place in the usual way at the public place of punishment.'

The Hermiones came for Pigot just after eleven that night. Among the first men into the captain's cabin was a

Dane, an Irishman, an American and a Cornishman. They carried tomahawks and cutlasses. Above them on the quarterdeck Lieutenant Foreshaw heard the killing below. He ordered William Turner, master's mate, to go below and see what was happening.

'If you want to know you can go down yourself,' said Turner.

Foreshaw realized they would have to change course and look for help from their sister ship, the *Diligence*, somewhere to windward in the dark night. Thomas Osborne was the man at the wheel. Lieutenant Foreshaw ordered him to put the helm up. Osborne replied, 'I'll see you damned first.'

Foreshaw hit Osborne. Out of the dark several Hermiones emerged and began chopping and slicing at Lieutenant Foreshaw. Foreshaw backed slowly towards the rail, streaming blood. Finally he could go no further, and fell over the side. He landed in the mizzen chains (planks sticking out from the side of the ship). Half an hour later he crawled back onto the deck, weak from loss of blood. The mutineers at first stepped back, as from a ghost. He spoke and they realized their mistake. They pitched him back over the side, and he passed out of history.

Captain Pigot went out his cabin window. James Allen found Lieutenant Douglas hiding under a cot. Allen was 14 years old and worked as Douglas's personal servant. As the men went for the lieutenant, Allen pushed forward with a tomahawk, crying 'Let me have a chop at him: he shan't make me jump about in the gunroom any more.' Midshipman John Smith was 13 years old and widely disliked. The Hermiones pushed him out a porthole.

The people took stock. They controlled the ship. The leaders met in the captain's cabin. Lawrence Cronin stood up to speak to the men: 'I have been a republican since the beginning of the war,' he said, and launched into a revolutionary speech. The people cheered wildly. At the end Cronin said they should kill all the remaining officers. 'Pass them up, pass them up,' was the cry. The surgeon (Cronin's boss), the purser, the first lieutenant, the captain's clerk, the boatswain and the marine officer went into the Caribbean.

Among the officers only the master, the carpenter, the gunner and Midshipman Casey remained alive. These men were liked: the master's servant boy was going through the ship in tears pleading with the men for his boss's life; Casey had been flogged by Pigot only a little while before. The moderates among the leaders insisted on a vote. A forest of hands went up for mercy.

The *Hermione* ran for the Spanish Main – enemy territory. They landed in what is now Venezuela. The four surviving officers gave themselves up as prisoners of war. So did one loyalist among the ship's company. The remaining 150 or so men changed their names and looked for work or a passage to the United States. The only woman on board was the wife of the murdered boatswain. She chose to go with the mutineers.

For the next 20 years the Admiralty pursued the Hermiones with a fierce vengeance. Many of the men continued to 'use the sea' for they had to work to eat, and it was their only trade. Eventually 33 Hermiones were caught, and 24 of them were hanged. The four officers who survived testified again and again at these courts martial, sending to the gallows men who had voted to save their lives.

Lawrence Cronin, the revolutionary, settled in Venezuela. Almost 120 other mutineers got clean away.[2]

The mutiny on the *Hermione* has everything: a sadistic captain, a bloody rising, the men running for the Spanish

Main and the Admiralty in cruel pursuit. In fact, it was the only mutiny in 22 years of war where the men killed the captain. Far more typical was the mutiny on the *Winchelsea* at Spithead in 1793.[3] It began with a letter from the ship's company to the admiral:

Winchelsea, Sper. 16th, 1793

Your Honour,

We now lay under the disagreeable opportunity of Informing Your Honour that our usage is not altogether as good as we formerly were used to in others of his Majesty's ships besides it has been heard openly for Captain Fisher that he will use us in a More Crewel Manner than ever he did which gives us a very dismal prospect of the Voyage we are going to proceed we are all with one accord willing to serve our King and Country upon any Demand Whatsoever but we are fully determined never to go to Sea under Capt. Fisher's command. French Prison will be more agreeable to us or Death alone than to be commanded by him We hope your Honour will Pity our Misfortune & give us Speedy Relief.

As our Situation at this Present time is Shocking to Repeat we all Remain With our Duty to our King.

Yours &c
Winchelseas.[4]

The letter was addressed to Sir Peter Parker, Commander in Chief at Spithead. The men were threatening to desert to the French without a fight.

Next morning they staged a demonstration.[5] The ship was riding at anchor. The boatswain piped all hands on deck to get out the ship's boats, but 44 of them remained below.

They used their hammocks and sea-chest to barricade themselves in the forward gun bay.

Captain Richard Fisher went below with one officer. The men stood with their backs to Fisher, and the darkness made it impossible for him to identify any individual. Captain Fisher threatened violence. He fired his pistol into the hammocks to underline his point. The people were unarmed, though the officer thought he saw a marlinspike gleam in the darkness. The Winchelseas refused to sail and demanded that Captain Fisher let them speak to the admiral. They said they could no longer tolerate the way they were used. They wanted a new ship and new officers, or individual transfers to other ships. Out of the dark an unidentifiable voice said, 'One and all now.' The people gave three cheers.

Fisher continued threatening. Finally the Winchelseas agreed that if the officers went up on deck they would follow. After ten minutes, and presumably a lot of argument, the men went on deck and reported for muster. It was the first mutiny of the war.

What is really interesting is what happened afterwards. Two seamen and a master's mate were court-martialled for mutiny. The evidence was thin. Generally only a few seamen ever testified against their mates in mutiny trials. On the *Winchelsea* nobody did. Every witness from below decks told the same story: he personally had been forced to stay below, and he had recognized none of his shipmates among the 43 men with him. The master's mate was acquitted. The two seamen were convicted only of 'being concerned in the said mutiny, that being present thereat, they did not use their utmost Endeavour to suppress the same'. Accordingly on 7 October William Price and William Duggan were flogged round the fleet. Price took 131 lashes and Duggan 141 before they could take no more.[6] It was no picnic, but it was not the noose. It was the usual penalty for desertion, not for leading a mutiny.

The floggings did not solve the admiral's problem. In their letter the Winchelseas had said they were 'fully determined' and effectively threatened to surrender to the French. There was no way of knowing if they would carry out this threat. Four days after the mutiny Captain Fisher wrote to the admiral. He said he had found 73 petty officers and able seamen, as well as two ordinary seamen, who wanted a transfer. Fisher wanted them all exchanged into another ship.[7] We can assume he was unsure of his ability to control his crew.

Nine days after the floggings the *Winchelsea* discharged Fisher, eight petty officers and eight seamen into another ship. Their places were taken by ten seamen, eight petty officers and a new captain.[8]

The Winchelseas had won. Admiral Parker had removed the hated Captain Fisher and sixteen of his 'followers': eight foremen and eight of his 'fancy men'. Duggan and Price may have been brutally beaten. But mutiny had worked.

It had worked on the *Hermione*, too. Captain Pigot met a rough justice, and over four-fifths of the ship's company escaped. But the *Winchelsea* was far more typical. It was not an armed revolt. Like most mutinies, it was really a strike and a demonstration. In the armed forces of all ages such actions are called 'mutiny'.

Mutineers were sometimes desperate and always angry men. They were not fools. Like all strikers, sometimes they won and sometimes they lost. Their leaders were often brutally victimized. But on some ships, at some times, the people found heroes to lead them.

# 1

## 'The crew, too, by some means had the impression that my mother had brought me on board to get rid of me'

Samuel Leech was the son of servants on an English country estate. As a boy he constantly badgered his mother to let him go to sea. Finally she relented. He joined the Navy, carrying two going-away presents: a Bible and a pack of cards. During the War of 1812 he deserted to the Americans. He eventually opened a shop in New England, married a Connecticut Yankee, and gave up drink. He wrote his memoirs in 1842. When he described the organization of a ship his mind turned not to the country estates of his boyhood but to the new factories that were springing up all around him:

> This community [the ship's] is governed by laws peculiar to itself: it is arranged and divided in a manner suitable to its circumstances. Hence, when its members first come together, each one is assigned his respective station and duty . . . Each task has its man, and each man his place. A ship contains a set of *human* machinery, in which every man is a wheel, a band, or a crank, all moving with wonderful regularity and precision to the will of its machinist – the all-powerful captain.[1]

In the eighteenth century this set of 'human machinery' was unique. On a man-of-war 600 men worked and ate together under one command. These ships were among the largest workplaces in the world and, in many ways, were closer to a modern car factory than to the country house of Leech's boyhood.

The reason was the guns. The great ships were floating batteries and were described by the number of guns they carried. The usual battleship was a '74': it carried 74 guns. In turn, guns were called after the weight of shot they fired. So a '74' carried mainly '32 pounders' and '24 pounders'.[2]

The great ships were floating batteries. All available space was given over to housing their weaponry. For instance the *Victory* at Trafalgar carried 104 guns, 90 of these were on three gun decks. Each deck was about 186 feet long and 51 feet wide – in other words, the total area of all three decks was about half the size of a football field. The ships fought in a 'line-of-battle', the nose of one ship up against the tail of another. The line moved at the speed of the slowest ship.

Speed in itself was unimportant. What was crucial in the great sea fights was seamanship. Each fleet tried to tack to gain the weather advantage. Every admiral hoped for some captain on the other side to make a mistake and open a hole in the line. Then the nearest ship would break through the hole in the enemy line. Guns were carried in rows on either side of the ship. Half of them were fired in any one 'broadside'. But a ship was terribly vulnerable if an attacker broke the line and passed under the stern or across the bow. Then the attacker could deliver a full broadside. Each gun was aimed carefully and fired at pointblank range as the gun port passed the midline of the victim ship. At the 'Glorious First of June', for instance, the *Queen Charlotte* broke the French line and passed behind the *Jacobin*. One broadside killed or wounded 300 of the 600 men on the *Jacobin*, forcing the crippled ship to retire from the fight.[3]

The combination of men, guns and sails was crucial to frigates in a different way. Frigates carried smaller and fewer guns than a 74. So a single broadside from a 74 could blow them out of the water. By tradition the frigates in each fleet sat and watched the larger ships fight it out. Frigates were fast. They carried messages quickly from fleet to fleet. The British always had a few patrolling outside the French ports, ready to race home with a warning if the French fleet came out. Though smaller than a 74, the frigate was a terror to merchant shipping. Frigates chased down privateers and merchantmen alike.

There were many smaller ships in the Navy: bomb ships, sloops, brigs and tenders. The frigates and 74s were 'square rigged'. The smaller ships were rigged at least partly 'fore-and-aft' and could sail fast and close to the wind.

Twenty men could take a merchant ship across the Atlantic. A warship the same size carried 300. Again, the guns made the difference: ten to fourteen men for each pair of guns. Each gun also needed a woman or boy as 'powder monkey'.[4]

The demand for men was immense. Any 'landsman' could learn to work a gun or pull on a rope – indeed, the boatswain's mates would beat him until he did. But it took balance and experience for a 'topman' to take in the sails while hanging in the swinging rigging far above the deck. The quartermaster's mates took the wheel. The sailmaker's crew and the carpenter's crew were skilled men. Each gun needed a 'captain' who knew the job. Some of the 'waisters' could stand around the ship's waist pulling on ropes, but some of them had to know which ropes were which. Captain Marryat estimated that over a third of the crew had to be men 'bred to the sea'.[5]

In wartime the Navy grew by leaps and bounds, as did the

merchant marine. Because good seamen were in short supply, wages shot up. A sailor could make three or four times as much in a merchant ship as in the Navy. And he was far surer of actually receiving his wages.

Perhaps it would have made no difference anyway if the Navy had paid decent rates. Sailors hated the brutality and boredom of the man-of-war. No experienced seaman joined willingly. John Bechervaise, for instance, was a Guernseyman from a seafaring family and seafaring island. He first went to sea in 1803. Seventeen years later, in the spring of 1820, Bechervaise found himself in London. He could not find a berth in any ship and had a wife and children to feed:

I looked round the docks. Nothing was stirring . . . In my rambles I saw men who had been to my knowledge masters and chief mates of vessels, who would now gladly have gone before the mast: to paint the distress that pervaded every part of the merchant service is beyond my power. The immense number of men discharged from ships of war who had foolishly spent their money and now got into deep distress strolling about the streets, some begging, others worse, was truly painful to those who possessed any feeling . . . Of all the places then dreaded by seamen in the merchant service, a ship of war is the worst. I fully had my share of the prejudice, but there was no alternative . . . Painful indeed was the parting from my home. May the 6th, 1820, early in the morning, I passed by the R——, then fitting out, and for the first time in my life saw the monstrous fabric that was to be my residence for several years, with a shudder of grief I cannot describe.[6]

Bechervaise was a volunteer, and no malcontent. Having joined as a petty officer he was soon promoted to quartermaster. He loved the sight of a trim deck with the brasswork gleaming. While proud of the Navy his 'prejudice' is echoed by every other seaman who left his memoirs.[7]

James Durand, for instance, was an American impressed into the Royal Navy. When the War of 1812 began he tried and failed to join the American prisoners-of-war who were taken out of the Navy and sent to Dartmoor prison: 'In fine, all those who went to prison were the best off. They were not flogged as often.' Samuel Leech (the boy with a Bible and a pack of cards) records: 'The crew, too, by some means had an impression that my mother had brought me on board to get rid of me, and therefore bestowed their bitterest curses on her in the most profuse manner imaginable.'[8]

It is impossible to tell what proportion of a ship's company were pressed men. The ships' books show about half as pressed – clearly an understatement. Many pressed men took the 'bounty' when they joined and went into the books as 'volunteer'. Some men, like Bechervaise, were reluctant volunteers. Some were sent as volunteers by the magistrates. In theory it was illegal to press foreigners. So all such men were signed up as volunteers.

The matter is well summed up by John Nicol, who had joined as a boy: 'I was surprised to see so few, who, like myself, had chosen it for the love of that line of life.'[9]

Even enthusiasts often regretted their decision. Jack Nastyface volunteered and was taken by tender to the Nore:

Upon getting on board this vessel, we were ordered down in the hold, and the gratings were put over us; as well as a guard of marines placed around the hatchway with their muskets loaded and fixed bayonets, as though we had been culprits of the first degree, or capital convicts. In this place we spent the day and following night huddled together, for there was not room to stand or sit separate; . . . some were sea-sick, some retching, others were smoking, whilst many were so overcome by the stench, that they fainted for want of air.

But it was too late for Nastyface to change his mind.[10]

Just before Trafalgar, Nelson ran up his famous signal to the fleet: 'England expects every man will do his duty.' England did not expect it only of the English, however, for they formed barely half the fleet. The Irish were the next largest group. There were also many Scots and a large number of blacks from the West Indies and the American south. Blacks were among the few sailors who preferred the Navy to where they had come from. Many Americans were pressed into the fleet.

The English felt they somehow owned all these nationalities. On top of this about a tenth of the fleet were 'true foreigners' from countries never under English rule. During these wars many Frenchmen served in the English fleet – and many Englishmen in the American and French fleets.

The Navy had an insatiable need for warm bodies. The press gang fed this appetite from every port and every merchant ship unlucky enough to come across a man-of-war. In 1812 the United States finally went to war to stop the Royal Navy stealing her sailors (the Americans also thought they could grab Canada).

Edward Jackson was one of these American sailors. He was a free black man from Philadelphia. The press gang caught him in Liverpool in 1795. He was put on the tender

13

*Bruyton* with other men to be carried to the fleet. The volunteers were allowed to be on deck but the pressed men like Jackson were locked in the 'press room'. At night the volunteers seized the ship. They had been paid the recruitment bounty: so there was no reason to hang around. They seized muskets and threw the officer of the watch down the hatch. Then they released the press men and sailed the tender to shore and freedom.

Jackson was later caught with another man. He gave his name as 'Edward Jackson'. The court had difficulty accepting a black man with a surname and tried him for mutiny and desertion under the name 'Prince Edward the Black alias Jackson'. They asked him if he had anything to say in his defense. He had papers to show he was American with a wife and family in that country. He had carried a 'protection' – a letter from the American government stating that he could not be pressed – which he had shown to Mr. Cragg, the Press Master in Liverpool. Cragg had torn up the protection in front of his face:

> I asked him the reason why he tore it. He gave me
> no answer but took me along with him. I thought it
> very hard to be taken away in a foreign country,
> where I had neither friends nor relations to do
> anything for me.

Jackson and his mate were acquitted on the charge of mutiny and convicted of the lesser charge of desertion. Each man was sentenced to be flogged round the fleet: 300 lashes.[11]

The Navy took men where it could. Lieutenant Hodgskin disapproved:

In 1811, I knew Africans, who had been stolen from

Africa, taken in a slave-ship, afterwards cloathed, on board a guard-ship, and without being able to speak a word of English, sent to man the British fleet, to fight the battles of our country. Such a thing is a burlesque upon a national defense.[12]

Samuel Richardson, the gunner, remembered one shipmate. The fleet was carrying many soldiers. The young lord who commanded the soldiers met a lost-looking Scandinavian sailor on the docks. With a charming smile the young nobleman invited the sailor into his boat. The boat's crew rowed out to Richardson's ship and the man was pressed. They had to get his name, birthplace, and rating. To every question they asked he replied, 'Orla hou.' They supposed that in his language 'Orla hou' meant 'I don't understand you.' So they pressed him under the name 'Orla Hou'. When Richardson left the ship five years later the man was still on board. He spoke fluent English and was one of the best seamen in the ship's company. He still drew his pay in the name of 'Orla Hou'.[13]

The net result of such coercion was that 'a number of outraged individuals were collected in our fleets'.[14] There they immediately learned to hate the driving regime of work. Leech describes it well:

The great disparity of numbers between the crew of a merchant ship and that of a man of war, occasions a difference in their internal arrangement and mode of life, scarcely conceivable by those who have not seen both. This is seen throughout, from the act of rousing the hands in the morning to that of taking in sail. In the merchantman, the watch below is called up by a few strokes of the handspike on the

15

forecastle; in the man of war by the boatswain and his mates . . . You immediately hear a sharp, shrill whistle; this is succeeded by another from his mates. Then follows his hoarse, rough cry of 'All hands ahoy!' which is forthwith repeated by his mates. Scarcely has this sound died upon the ear, before the cry of 'Up all hammocks away!' succeeds it, to be repeated in like manner . . . No delay is permitted, for as soon as the above-mentioned officers have uttered their imperative commands, they run below, each armed with a rope's end, with which they belabor the shoulders of any luckless wight upon whose eyes sleep yet hangs heavily, or whose slow-moving limbs show him to be but half-awake.

With a rapidity which would surprise a landsman, the crew dress themselves, lash their hammocks and carry them on deck, where they are stowed for the day. There is a system even in this arrangement; every hammock has its appropriate place . . .

A similar rapidity attends the performance of every duty. The word of command is given in the same manner, and its prompt obedience is enforced by the same ceremonious rope's-end. To skulk is therefore next to impossible: the least tardiness is rebuked by the cry of 'Hurrah my hearty! bear a hand! heave along! heave along!' This system of driving is far from agreeable; it perpetually reminds you of your want of liberty; it makes you feel, sometimes, as if the hardest crust, the most ragged garments, with the freedom of your own native hills, would be preferable to John Bull's 'beef and duff', joined as it is with the rope's end of the driving boatswain.[15]

As in any armed services, a lot of the work was cleaning. And a lot of it was make-work. All hands had to report before 4.30 a.m. to clean the decks. They finished just in time for breakfast at 6.30. Sentries made sure nobody could sneak back down the hatches. The men were on their knees scrubbing. A mishipman or mate stood in front of them, moving slowly backwards. He made sure no man advanced on his knees till his bit of deck was thoroughly scrubbed. Sailors hated cleaning the decks.[16]

Many captains spent hours drilling the men in the rigging and in gunnery. The speed of gunnery made all the difference in battle. But it was hard, hot work lugging the great guns in and out. And on no account were the men to fire the guns; the Admiralty counted every cannon ball. For instance, when Richardson was gunner he lost four cannon balls overboard in a storm. He went to the captain in a nervous sweat. The captain kindly told him not to worry; he was hoping for a battle soon. Then they could write off the four cannon balls.[17]

The driving regime angered seamen. So did corruption. King Charles II is said to have told his council one night: 'If ever you intend to man the fleet without being cheated by captains and pursers, you may go to bed.'[18]

The corruption of pursers was legendary. The purser bought all the stores and handed them out. He was a contractor in his own right. The post was bought and sold for large sums. All pursers paid for provisions at 16 ounces to the pound; they sold them to the men at 14 ounces to the pound. One of the main demands in the Spithead mutiny of 1797 was a 16-ounce pound.

Another demand in that mutiny was that surgeons stop stealing the medicines. It is not clear if surgeons were any more corrupt than, say, boatswains. Probably the men took a lenient view of redirecting a spare sail. But when there were no medicines they became incensed.

Like other workers of the time, sailors held a strong 'moral economy'. They knew their rights to proper rations and they were going to have them. On shore workers tended to blame merchants and middlemen for the high price of bread. Afloat, the captain was at the centre of any corruption: he signed the dishonest books; he ran the ship; he dealt with complaints; he told the men to shut up or be flogged when they complained about missing cheeses. The captain usually had some fiddles of his own on the go and took a cut of the others. Thus the men's anger about corruption and work focused on their boss: the captain.

The ship was a community of hostile groups. Officers and men understood this class system in terms of parts of the ship. They spoke of people as places. The officers as a whole were 'the quarterdeck'. The men were the 'focsle' (forecastle) or the 'lower deck'. Junior officers were 'midshipmen'.

Look at the diagram of a ship seen from the side, on page 19. No real ship was like this. They all had lots of odd little rooms and most of them had more decks. No ship with one gun deck would also have poop deck. Figure 1 is a social map. It shows the rough-and-ready way a sailor automatically divided any ship.

The sailors sleep forward on the gun deck. They play on the forecastle. They work in the tops: the foretop, the maintop and the mizzentop. The officers sleep aft on the main deck. They play and work aft on the quarterdeck. The sailor was sent to the masthead as a routine duty. The midshipman was 'mastheaded' as a punishment. As it happens, the rigging and the front of a sailing ship are the cold, wet part; the back is the warm and dry.

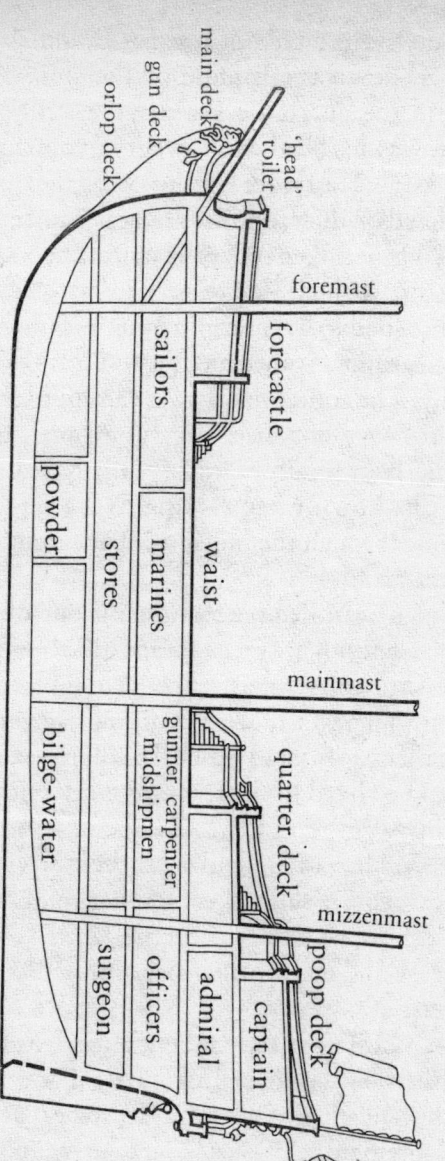

*Social organization on board*

orlop deck
gun deck
main deck
'head'
toilet

foremast

forecastle

sailors

powder

stores

marines

waist

mainmast

bilge-water

gunner carpenter
midshipmen

quarter deck

mizzenmast

surgeon

officers

admiral

captain

poop deck

These divisions were not just for sleeping. A frontier of control ran down the middle of the ship. A sailor with business on the quarterdeck always stood on the leeward side. That way his head was lower than the captain's on the windward side. Nastyface was 'never on the quarterdeck but when ordered on duty, and was only permitted to say "Aye, Aye, sir", when spoken to, at the same time touching the rim of my castor, with all due respect to my officers.'[19]

Nastyface had to be careful. Sometimes men did come aft singly or in groups. Sometimes the result was a court martial for mutiny. The court was always careful to find out if such men had behaved in a disrespectful manner. Had so and so talked quietly or loudly? Did he really have his cap in hand and eyes cast down when talking to the captain or had he merely gone through the motions? The wrong answer could cost a man his life.

Many men patrolled the frontier of control. The first line were the 'captains': the 'captain of the maintop', the 'captain of the mizzenmast', the 'captain of the forecastle' and so on. These men were working gangers. They were skilled at their craft, held a moral authority and did not beat the men. They lived in the forward berth with the men and in a mutiny went with them.

The second line of control were the warrent officers: the cooper, carpenter, sailmaker, gunner, and surgeon. They lived amidships, between officers and men . They sometimes beat the men and in a mutiny they almost always went with the officers.

Any 'captain' or officer facing a recalcitrant man could call for the boatswain or his mates. Their main job was driving the landsmen. They would also beat any man singled out by a foreman or officer. The boatswain's mates might mess with the men, but they wielded the cat-o'-nine-tails at formal floggings. In a mutiny the boatswain went with the officers; his mates could go either way.

If a man got cheeky the boatswain could call for the ship's corporal or the master-at-arms. In a crisis he yelled for the marines, the major repressive force on board. In battle the marines manned the guns like everybody else, just as in landings they fought side by side with the sailors.

Their main task, however, was not to make landings or board other ships. In any confrontation the captain immediately called the marines to accompany him below decks. Their weapons cowed the sailors and they arrested the trouble-makers

Officers valued the marines. Captain Glascock wrote, 'In such a crisis, every officer must be keenly sensible of the vital importance and inestimable value of a few loyal and courageous hearts.'

On most days the marines did no work but sentry duty. At night they slept between the officers and men. For formal floggings, however, the people were drawn up on the main deck. The officers stood above them on the quarterdeck. The marines stood with the officers and levelled their muskets down towards the main deck, the powder already in the pan.

Two statistics show just how tense life was on a man of war. At the height of the war the Navy had 20,000 marines and 110,000 sailors. On a man of war with a crew of 600, almost 100 of them would be marines. Their sole purpose, between engagements, was to keep the men in order.

This strict frontier of control separated officers and men. Within their own space, forward and between the decks, the sailors were able to build and subtly defend a world of their own. There they created a counter-culture of the forecastle, centred on women, drink and solidarity. The ships were full of women in port and awash with drink at all times, as Chapter 7 describes in greater detail. For the moment it is only necessary to remember that sailors had their own private world. Solidarity was at its heart. Other sailors were your mates: 'shipmates', 'berthmates', 'messmates'. Both officers and men spoke of sailors as 'the people' of the ship. The men of *Hermione*, for instance, thought of themselves as a collective: the Hermiones. In what follows we shall encounter many such collectives.

# 2

## 'If there were no punishment for selling their clothes, the men would soon be naked'

Work produced constant tension. Because the officers felt that the men would not start work on their own, the boatswain's mates had to 'start' them. Lieutenant Hodgskin describes them starting as

> one man beating another with a piece of rope as hard as he can hit him: the other being perfectly defenseless, and forbid him even to look displeased, as that is contempt or disrespect . . . Starting is more generally used for want of alacrity than for any other crime.
>
> In hoisting the topsails to the mast-head, hoisting boats in and out, hoisting in beer and water, and such like duties, when they are not done with smartness, the captain stationed a boatswain's mate at different parts of the deck, each with a rope's end, with orders to beat every man as he passed . . . In performing all the little pieces of duty, every man, almost, as he ran and pulled upon the rope, had to pass . . . Thus, whether good or bad, whether old or young, whether exerting himself or not, nearly every man in the ship got a beating.[1]

The rope's end might be two inches in diameter. It might be a halyard eight inches thick. Some boatswain's mates used bamboo canes instead. Sometimes a starting was a full beating rather than a passing thwack. An angry boatswain's mate might lay into a man as he danced around to avoid the blows. Or a cranky officer could order a beating.

Midshipmen were often the worst disciplinarians. Nasty-face remembered one who

> was a youth not more than twelve or thirteen years of age; but I have often seen him get on the carriage of a gun, call a man to him, and kick him about the thighs and body, and with his fist would beat him about the head; and these, although prime seamen, at the same time dared not demur.

When the midshipman fell in battle at Trafalgar, 'the general exclamation was, *"Thank God we are rid of the young tyrant"*.'[2]

James Durand, on the other hand, reports that his midshipmen asked the men to stoop so the boys could beat them. Lieutenant Hodgskin, himself once a midshipman, thought their viciousness came from being taken away from their families so young and not receiving a proper education on board:

> If any man is not convinced, I can only wish him to go on board ship, and see the hours of the midshipmen alternately employed, sleeping, playing and walking the decks, with their hands in their pockets, that he may hear their conversation and see their amusements; and, if he would afterwards make them judges of the actions of men, I should pronounce him *mad*.[3]

Such summary beatings accounted for the overwhelming majority of punishments. But when a captain got really angry he was supposed to wait until the next day for a formal flogging. Captain Glascock describes why in his book of advice for young officers:

> An indulgence, therefore, in passion, under circumstances of disappointment, mistake, or mishap, should be rigidly repressed, which, whilst the paroxysm lasts, tends to the debasement of those who are its objects, and robs its subject of either reflection or the free exercise of the native faculties of the mind. If an anecdote were wanting to exemplify one of the fatal consequences of unrestrained passion, it would only be necessary to refer to the melancholy fate of the captain of *La Revolutionnaire* who, sailing under sealed order, fell on the deck in a fit of anger at some of the crew, and on being carried below, expired.[4]

Punishment came in all shapes and sizes. But the word 'punishment' meant one thing: flogging. The cat-o'-nine-tails was the symbolic heart of discipline, and a formal flogging was *the* ceremony of power. Samuel Leech describes the ritual on the *Macedonian*:

> A poor fellow had fallen into a very sailor-like offence of getting drunk. For this the captain sentenced him to the punishment of four dozen lashes. He was first placed in irons all night . . . until the captain bade the first lieutenant prepare the hands to witness the punishment. Upon this the lieutenant transmitted the order to the master-at-arms. He then ordered the grating or hatch of square holes to be rigged: it was placed accordingly between the main and spar [i.e. quarter] decks, not far from the mainmast.

While these preparations were going on, the officers were dressing themselves in full uniform and arming themselves with their dirks. The prisoner's messmates carried him his best clothes, to make him appear in as decent a manner as possible. This is always done, in the hope of moving the feelings of the captain favourably towards the prisoner.

This done, the hoarse, dreaded cry of 'All hands ahoy to witness punishment!' from the lips of the boatswain, peals along the ship as mournfully as the notes of a funeral knell. At this signal the officers muster on the spar deck, the men on the main deck. Next came the prisoner, guarded by a marine on one side and the master-at-arms on the other, he was marched up to the grating. His back was made bare, and his shirt laid loosely upon his back. The two quarter-masters proceeded to seize him up, that is, they tied his hands and feet with spun yarns, called the seizings, to the grating. The boatswain's mates, whose office is to flog on board a man-of-war, stood ready with their dreadful weapon of punishment, the cat-o'-nine-tails. This instrument of torture was composed of nine cords, a quarter of an inch round, and about two feet long, the ends whipt with fine twine. To these cords was affixed a stock, two feet in length, covered with red baize. The reader may be sure that it is a most formidable instrument in the hands of a strong, skilful man. Indeed, any man who would whip his horse with it would commit an outrage on humanity, which the moral feeling of any community would not tolerate; he would be prosecuted for cruelty; yet it is used to whip MEN on board ships of war.

The boatswain's mate is ready, with coat off, and whip in hand. The captain gives the word. Carefully spreading the cords with the fingers of his left hand, the executioner throws the cat over his right shoulder; it is brought down upon the now uncovered herculean shoulders of the MAN. His flesh creeps – it reddens as if blushing at the indignity; the sufferer groans; lash follows lash, until the first mate, wearied with the cruel employment, give place to a second. Now two dozen of these dreadful lashes have been inflicted: the lacerated back looks inhuman; it resembles roasted meat burnt nearly black before a scorching fire; yet still the lashes fall; the captain continues merciless. Vain are the cries and prayers of the wretched man. 'I would not forgive the Saviour,' was the blasphemous reply of one of these naval demi-gods, or rather demi-fiends, to a plea for mercy.

The executioners keep on. Four dozen strokes have cut up his flesh, and robbed him of all self-respect; there he hangs, a pitied, self-despised groaning, bleeding wretch; and now the captain cries, Forbear! His shirt is thrown over his shoulders; the seizings are loosed; he is led away, staining his path with red drops of blood, and the hands, 'piped down' by the boatswain, sullenly return to their duties.[5]

Sometimes the hands were more than sullen. Just below the surface of their faces the ship's company seethed. At times they greeted each stroke with a moaning so low that no one man could be accused of it. At times they did more. On the *Victorious* the prisoner turned to the ship's company and said 'By God I will not strip.' It appears that the captain did not dare force him but left it to a subsequent court-martial to award 150 lashes.[6]

In June 1802, the marines were drawn up on the quarterdeck of the *Audacious*. In a low but clear voice marine Joseph Hawkes said, 'It's a damned shame.' Another marine was pulled out of line. The captain slugged him and he was put into irons. Next morning he was taken up on to the quarterdeck, where he said it wasn't him, it was Hawkes. The court martial awarded Hawkes 300 lashes.[7]

Flogging was a tense ceremony, a time when officers watched the men carefully. On the *America* in 1795 the sailors were lining up to witness punishment. For reasons that are unclear, they stood in rows with fixed bayonets. Lieutenant Lake felt that Samuel Beech had been slow in lining up, so he began beating him with a stick. Beech turned to face his tormentor, who raised his sword to ward off an anticipated blow from the sailor. Another seaman, Joseph Collier, made a remark over his shoulder to Beech without turning round. At this point Lake panicked. He had both Beech and Collier immediately arrested. The court martial acquitted both of them.[8]

A flogging was not always the end of the punishment. Captain Glascock, in his manual for young officers, advises that:

The moment the painful duty is ended, no
inclination should be shown to keep the recollection
of it alive by any ill-timed comment, or intimation
(which, unfortunately, is too much the habit with
many, in other respects, very judicious officers), that
in addition to his punishment the delinquent is set
down in the captain's private list. The tendency of
such an intimation is to make men reckless of the

future, and regardless of character, which they, with a good deal of reason, imagine is irrevocably lost the moment their name is enrolled in writing on that hateful memorial, emphatically denominated by sailors the '*Black List*'. No unprofitable task in the way of black-list duty should ever be imposed. It is in the recollection of many, that captains have compelled seamen on this list to brighten the 'breeches of the guns', the 'belaying pins', the ring bolts in the desk, and even a two-and thirty-pound shot, tasks which the sailor must himself perceive were useless.[9]

Glascock was writing in 1826, 11 years after the end of the war. He noted that such practices were gradually dying out in the Royal Navy. They were, however, becoming newly popular in the American Navy, particularly on the smarter ships in the Mediterranean.

Captain Glascock may not have been typical of officers of his generation – sometimes he seems a bit soft. For instance, he was against putting men in irons:

A man of spirit will naturally brood over and repine at the unnecessary disgrace thus inflicted for trifling offences. The injurious consequences of resorting to irons in the latter case may be most aptly exemplified by referring to numerous well-known instances, where a string of men, whose offences have been trifling have been exhibited, each bolted by the leg on the half-deck, or other most exposed part of the ship, whilst visitors from the shore have been conducted round the vessel by their own officers. [One imagines that many of these visitors were of the 'fairer sex'.] A sailor must be made of stone not to feel keenly such ill-timed degradation. The sentiment is not confined to the prisoner: an inference is drawn by the visitant . . . most discreditable to the character of the seamen and respectability of the service. Thus the injury is twofold; at once inflicting on the sailor unnecessary degradation and pain, whilst it serves the malignant purposes of malcontents on shore to calumniate the character of that constitutional force, which has hitherto been, and will ever continue, the natural bulwark of these sea-girt isles.[10]

A formal flogging was designed to terrify the sailors. The pomp, the ritual, the dress uniforms, the regulated and rhythmic brutality – all contributed to the same effect. But how did it feel to the flogged man?

Flogging was shameful, and few men have left records of their experiences. One man recalled 'Nothing but an O, a few O my Gods, and then you can put on your shirt.' Another, a soldier, flogged with the lighter military cat, wrote that after the first few strokes,

> The pain in my lung was more severe, I thought, than on my back. I felt as if I would burst in the internal parts of my body . . . I put my tongue between my teeth, held it there, and bit it in almost two pieces. What with the blood from my tongue, and my lips, which I had also bitten, and the blood from my lungs, or some other internal part, ruptured by the writhing agony, I was almost choked, and became black in the face.[11]

Punishments varied enormously. A court martial would award a deserter 100 to 300 lashes. A captain could give him a quick two dozen and have done with it. The captain had great discretion. The law said he could not award more than a dozen without a court martial and twelve lashes is indeed the most common punishment recorded in the logs. But on occasion every captain awarded more and noted the fact in the official logs. A few men got away with half a dozen: many got two dozen. Some captains awarded three or four dozen regularly; 63 and 72 lashes were not unheard of.[12]

Flogging sometimes killed. This did not have much to do with the number of lashes, and most victims died some time afterwards. Many men survived 200 lashes. Some died after 36. Why?

The soldier quoted above remembered pain in the chest and blood from the lungs. One blow with a naval cat would knock down a standing man. The prisoner was lashed to a grating, and each blow slammed him against it. The historian and novelist Dudley Pope has done an interesting experiment. He made a replica of an old cat, and nailed two inch by half inch pine across a grating. He broke the wood with one blow of the cat. So he tried inch by inch pine. He broke it on the second blow.[13]

The danger was that a broken rib could float loose and slice into the lung. This would be devastatingly painful and on an eighteenth-century ship a punctured lung could easily lead to a fatal infection.

When sailors remembered watching floggings, words like 'meat' and 'liver' kept springing to mind. Here again the danger was infection. Men would not die of the beating itself: they would die later of gangrene.[14]

But we should not exaggerate. The overwhelming majority of flogged men recovered. Nor did all witnesses feel flogging was dangerous. Captain Chamier wrote a novel called *Ben Brace, the Last of Nelson's Agamemnons*. Ben Brace says:

'As for corporal punishment – which means a little back-scratching – I think I may say that it could not be abolished without injury to the service.' He goes on to explain that the men would not work without terror. He was, of course, right. Every regime of forced labour requires the lash. Captain Glascock summed up the case for flogging in 1826: 'The materials of which our navy are formed are, like granite, principally valuable for their hard, tough, and lasting wear-and-tear quality.'[15]

Whatever the pain, what sailors hated most about the lash was the degradation. Leech describes the scene as his ship heads for home:

> Visions of an old fire-side, of many a humble hearth-stone, poor, but precious, flitted across the visions of our crew that night. Hardships, severe discipline, were for the time forgotten in the dreams of hope. Would that I could say that everything in every mind was thus absorbed in pleasure! There were minds that writhed under what is never forgotten. Like the scar, that time may heal, but not remove, the flogged man forgets not that he has been degraded; the whip, when it scarred the flesh, went farther; it wounded the spirit; it struck the *man*; it begat a sense of degradation he must carry with him to his grave. We had many such on board our frigate; their laugh sounded empty, and sometimes their look became suddenly vacant in the midst of hilarity. *It was the whip entering the soul anew*. But most of our crew were, for the time, happy. They were homeward bound.[16]

Men were flogged for many reasons. On the *Culloden* in 1793, for instance, men were punished for sleeping on watch, being drunk and disobedient, fighting, neglect of duty and attempted desertion. On 30 March 1795 James Warner got 12 lashes for 'skulking and neglect of duty'. On 11 June Robert Leekey got 24 lashes for 'drunkenness and sundry misdemeanours'. On 13 June Samuel Tickner received 12 lashes for selling his trousers.[17]

Selling your clothes was not an uncommon offence. Sailors were pressed in what they stood up in. The cold of the North Sea could kill a man without stout canvas clothes. So the purser gave the men clothes on credit and collected the money when they were paid. Often the Navy did not get around to paying the sailors for years at a time.

The men were allowed shore liberty in foreign ports where the captain felt they would not desert. Their needs ashore were few but strong. They had no money to meet them. If he could, a sailor smuggled his spare clothes ashore and sold them for the price of a good time on the Genoa docks. But it was difficult. Officers kept a close watch on men going ashore. They kept lists of the men's clothes and there were regular clothes counts. Sometimes a man must have sold what he stood up in. When he reported for the boat to take him back to the ship, his crime would be obvious: a flogging would follow the next day. This may seem harsh. But, as Captain Marryat said, 'If there were no punishment for selling their clothes, the men would soon be naked.'[18]

The two most common offences were drunkenness and 'neglect of duty'. 'Neglect of duty' meant making a mistake. Lieutenant Hodgskin explains:

I have heard it avowed as a principle, by an officer of the highest reputation in His Majesty's service, and I have seen it acted upon, 'that no such thing as

33

an accident could happen'; consequently, any misfortune must have arisen in some person's neglect, and some person must be punished to prevent its recurrence. . . [Hodgskin goes on to give examples.] Some of the iron allotted to a man to polish does not shine well; his hammock has not been clean scrubbed; his clothes have wanted mending; his shirt has been dirty; or perhaps he may have neglected the captain's stock, or the wardroom dinner: These, and a thousand similar trifles, are what seamen are flogged for, as neglect of duty.[19]

It might seem hard to flog a man for drunkenness – after all, each day the Navy gave a man a gallon of beer or eight double rums. Like as not the officer who charged him had already had his grog and then a bottle or two of wine in the wardroom to wash it down. But men were not usually punished for such gentle social sipping. 'Drunkenness' meant the sort of falling-down drunk achieved by smuggling or hoarding drink.

Close behind drunkenness and neglect came floggings for talking back and looking surly. This offence was variously called 'disobedience', 'contempt', 'disrespect', 'insolence' or even 'mutinous behaviour'. It was particularly likely to happen when a drunken officer confronted a sailor himself three sheets to the wind. The angry sailor would fall naturally into obscenities and sometimes into threats. But a man could be punished for much less. According to Hodgskin:

It is not uncommon in the Navy for looks to be punished as contempt, for a claim to justice, as a right belonging to every member of society, for a protestation of innocence, particularly if supported by reasoning, against the rash intuitive convictions of a superior, to be punished at this enlightened period of the world as disrespect.[20]

The ships' logs show great variation in punishments. Some ships record at least one flogging a week; others can go a month without punishment. Where one officer swore at a man another would order two dozen lashes.

The key officers were the captain and the first lieutenant. The captain had the power to order floggings, but the first lieutenant was in charge of the day-to-day running of the ship. Furthermore, captains spent a lot of time on shore. Nastyface hated his 'old woman of a captain' for being constantly away in London at parties or in the House of Commons. (His captain doubled as an MP.) He left control to the tyrannical first lieutenant. Even when on board the captain 'flogged every man that was reported to him by the . . . lieutenant, without enquiring into the complaint, for that would have been beneath his dignity as a man and an officer'.[21]

It was always a tense time when the ship changed officers. The men waited to see which way the fresh wind blew. A new captain or first lieutenant might be a harsh flogger. Just as important, he would set the style for every boatswain's mate with a rope's end. Leech remembered one unpleasant surprise:

While in port we experienced a change of officers by no means agreeable to the crew. Mr. Scott, our first lieutenant, an amiable man, decidedly hostile to the practice of flogging, left us; for what cause, we could not ascertain. His successor, Mr. Hope, though bearing a very pleasant name, was an entirely different person . . . He was harsh, severe, and fond of seeing the men flogged. Of course, floggings became more frequent therefore; for although a lieutenant cannot flog upon his own authority, yet, such is the influence he exerts over a captain, that he has the utmost opportunity to gratify a thirst for punishment.'[22]

Such sadists were a minority among captains, but firm floggers were the norm. Nastyface reports that in his fleet of nine ships there were two kind captains. Perhaps that was about average. At the end of the voyage both kind captains received presents of gold plate or cups, bought with pennies contributed by the crew: it was one of the few ways they could express their appreciation formally. The seven floggers commanded men slow in their movements, broken in spirit, and always bad-mouthing the captain.[23]

Everybody appreciated a good officer. Even Leech remembered Lieutenant Scott with admiration:

Punishment leads to revenge, revenge to punishment. What is intended to cure, only aggravates the disease; the evil enlarges under the remedy; voluntary subordination ceases; gloom overspreads the crew; fear fills the breasts of the officers; the ship becomes a miniature of the house of fiends. While, on the other hand, mild regulations, enforced without an appeal to brute force, are easily carried into operation. The sailor has a warm heart; show him personal kindness, treat him as a man, he will then be a man; he will do anything for a *kind* officer. He will peril his life for him, nay, he will cheerfully rush between him and danger. This was done at Tripoli, when the brave James offered his own arm to receive the fell stroke of a Turkish scimitar, aimed at the life of the bold Decatur, on board the frigate *Philadelphia*.[24]

The average captain was neither kind nor blood-thirsty. Lieutenant Hodgskin's captain was probably typical: a decent and religious man, he tried his best for the service, but he had been brought up to be a 'smart' officer.

I have seen this captain flog, I think, twenty-six men, part of them by candle-light, at both gangways, because their hammocks were not properly cleaned.

The number of men is stated from memory, as not thinking, at that time, it would ever become a duty to state it, and reason upon it to the public; and not being a spy upon any man's action, I made no note of the affair, however I might think it cruel; neither do I remember the amount of the lashes, but I am certain they were not less than one dozen each man.

The only time the men were allowed for scrubbing was one hour and a half during the night; in this time they had their hammocks, half a week's dirty clothes, and perhaps, a bag to scrub. It was not because they had not been scrubbed at all, but because they did not look well: I should say it was flogging men for impossibilities. It was in a warm climate, and, in a warm climate before, this captain had seen such things done; he would allow of no relaxation whatever, justly observing, if he began to relax, he knew not where to stop.[25]

The people had one ready remedy for a brutal captain: desertion. They called it 'running', a word which sounds better than 'desertion'. Most sailors were pressed men with little desire to stay on board. They were allowed ashore in foreign ports because relatively few deserted there. But in home ports the sentries kept a constant watch and the ship's boats rowed around to make sure nobody swam ashore. The punishment if a man was caught was terrifying. But on an unhappy ship escape from certain hell now outweighed the threat of hell later. Men ran from every ship every month, but a brutal captain increased the rate.

Nastyface says that his captain was so plagued by desertions that he had to recruit 2,100 men in two years to fill 600 places. He may have exaggerated, but desertion was a fact of life. Some men swam ashore in the dark. Even the trusted oarsmen in the captain's boat jumped onto the quay. Some men got their friends and relatives on shore to arrest them for debt and then paid off the debt after the ship had left. A boat's crew would row the lieutenant back to the ship, watch him jump for the side, and then row like hell for the shore. At Bantry Bay, Ireland, in 1814

the men were so determined, that they walked down the side of the ship, in presence of the sentinel at the gangway, and of the officer of the watch, took possession of one of the ship's boats, and notwithstanding they were fired at with ball-cartridges, persisted in their attempt, and ultimately succeeded in gaining the shore.[26]

The great majority of deserters got clean away. Since only a minority were caught, their punishment had to be all the fiercer to cow their mates. Jack Nastyface explains what this meant:

While lying at Spithead, in the year 1809 or 1810, four impressed seamen attempted to make their escape from a frigate, then lying there; one of their shipmates, a Dutchman, to whom they had entrusted the secret, betrayed their intention, and informed the commanding officer of their designs. They were tried by a court-martial, and sentenced to receive three hundred lashes, each through the fleet. On the first day after the trial that the weather was moderate enough to permit, the signal was made for a boat from each ship, with a guard of marines, to attend the punishment.

The man is placed in a launch, i.e. the largest ship's boat, under the care of the master-at-arms and a doctor. There is a capstan bar rigged fore and aft, to which this poor fellow is lashed by his wrists, and for fear of hurting him – humane creatures – there is a stocking put over each, to prevent him from tearing the flesh in his agonies. When all is ready, the prisoner is stript and seized to the capstan bar.

Punishment commences by the officer, after reading the sentence of the court-martial, ordering the boatswain's mates to do their duty. The cat-of-nine-tails is applied to the bare back, and at about every six lashes, a fresh boatswain's mate is ordered to relieve the executioner of this duty, until the prisoner has received, perhaps, twenty-five lashes: he is then cast loose, and allowed to sit down with a blanket rolled round him, is conveyed to the next ship, escorted by this vast number of armed boats, accompanied by that doleful music, 'The Rogue's March'.

In this manner he is conveyed from ship to ship, receiving alongside of each a similar number of stripes with the cat, until the sentence is completed.

It often, nay generally, happens, that nature is unable to sustain it, and the poor fellow faints and sinks under it, although every kind method is made use of to enable him to bear it, by pouring wine down his throat. The doctor will then feel his pulse, and often pronounces that the man is unable to bear more.

He is then taken, most usually insensible, to what is termed the *sick bay*; and, if he recovers, he is told he will have to receive the remainder of his punishment. When there are many ships in the fleet at the time of court-martial, this ceremony, if the prisoner can sustain it, will last nearly half the day.

On the blanket being taken from his back, and he supported or lifted to be lashed to the capstan-bar, after he has been alongside of several ships, his back resembles so much putrified liver, and every stroke of the cat brings away the congealed blood; and the boatswain's mates are looked at with the eye of a hawk to see they do their duty, and clear the cat's tail after every stroke, the blood at the time streaming through the fingers.[27]

The Admiralty clearly intended that every man who contemplated desertion should see such scenes in his dreams. Terror does not always work, however. The above quotation is from a book published in 1836 in London by a printer from Cheapside named William Robinson. Robinson was Nastyface himself. It was too risky to put his own name down as author. He was a deserter.[28] The book's full title is as set out on the title page:

# NAUTICAL ECONOMY

*or*

*Forecastle Recollections*

*of*

Events During the Last War

DEDICATED

*to the*

BRAVE TARS OF OLD ENGLAND

by a Sailor

Politely Called by the Officers of the Navy,

JACK NASTYFACE.

# 3

## 'I have an old mother who has not seen me for eight years'

Individuals and small groups could run from an unhappy ship. In addition there was always the possibility of collective action. Nobody – officers or people – ever forgot this.

The most common form of protest was writing a letter. The officers usually called them 'anonymous letters'. But they were not the work of an angry or twisted individual. They were signed by 'Eurydice Ship's Company' or 'Marines of the Bellerephon'.[1] They were letters from the people as a whole.

The people chose a sailor with good penmanship and style to write for them. Sometimes he wrote in the carpenter's store room or an officer's empty cabin, hidden from prying hostile eyes. But letters were not secret. The men had little real privacy from each other. Often the writer worked between the hammocks, consulting the whole company on the wording.

The sailors sent their letters to some powerful and possibly sympathetic man. If they had a cruel lieutenant and a kind captain, they wrote to the captain about the lieutenant and threw the letter on to the quarterdeck at night. Usually they wrote to the admiral about the captain and gave the letter to a prostitute to mail on shore. Where they thought the admiral useless, they wrote direct to the Admiralty office in London.

Working people on shore were always writing petitions to powerful people, for British society was a complex web of corruption. If you could get to the right man, he could fix anything. The sailors' letters had the same tone as these petitions: respectful, even crawling. Nevertheless, on both ship and shore there was always a silent threat behind any letter from a group of workers: We are together. We are organized. We stick by each other: you will not find out who wrote this. If you don't redress our grievances, there may be trouble.[2]

The *Bellerephon* provides an example. On 29 September 1795 nine marines were tried for 'attempting to make mutiny amongst the whole party on board, by complaining of harsh and improper treatment . . . and being accessory to the writing of a publick letter.'[3]

At the root of the matter was a grievance over job description. Marines were supposed to do sentry duty and nothing else. But those on the *Bellerephon* had to do a lot of the sailors' work. They even had to clean the decks. While they did it the boatswain's mates abused them. So they wrote to the marine commandant on shore asking for a transfer.

It was a polite letter. The shore commandant told Major Walker Smith, captain of marines on the *Bellerephon*, to look into it. Unfortunately, somebody traced the handwriting to marine John Cook. He was summoned to the quarterdeck. Faced with the evidence, he broke down and agreed to testify against his mates at a court-martial. This was most unusual.[4]

Cook was transferred to another ship immediately. The officers probably thought he would be happier there, and perhaps remain in better health. At the trial Cook said the whole marine company had been in favour of writing the letter. He named nine men whose berths were near his.

Cook said everybody had told him their objections. Then he summarized them in the letter. The other marines had told him that letter writing was often done. In his evidence the marine commandant confirmed this. He said that he gave the letter to Walker Smith to investigate. He thought no more of it for he received many such letters. At this point one of the judges took fright and asked the commandant if he meant that the marines on different ships in the fleet were conspiring to write similar letters. The commandant reassured him that all the letters were on different subjects.

The prosecutor at the trial was Lord Cranston, the captain of the *Bellerephon*. The usual string of officers testified. They said Lord Cranston was 'very sweet' to the marines. He was 'particularly kind and open' to the marines whenever he had them flogged at the gangway.

Then Walker Smith, the captain of marines, testified. He was discreet and carefully ambiguous. But he made it clear that he and the first lieutenant hated each other. He allowed the court to understand that the lieutenant was persecuting the marines to get at him. Walker Smith also said they were the finest body of men he had ever commanded. They had fought with great bravery when released from irons as the ship went into battle. The court took the hint. They convicted the nine marines, but declined to punish them. Instead, the court admonished them not to write letters again.

This case shows how letters normally worked. Lord Cranston scented organized discontent and charged the men with 'attempting to make a mutiny'. The letter, however, did not threaten mutiny, and some officers even approved of the complaint. The court did not think it was mutiny.

We seldom have such a window on the writing of letters. Although an enormous number were written,[5] very few of their authors were brought to trial – on average one or two a year in the whole Navy. We can see why from the case of Bryant McDonough.[6]

McDonough was a seaman on the *Eurydice* in 1796. He wrote a letter for the Eurydices to the Admiralty, complaining about First Lieutenant Colville. Colville had them cleaning the decks from four in the morning. If a man took any rest, he was struck in the face. He then bled on the 'holystone': the prayer-book-shaped rough stone used to clean the deck. Colville made the delinquent wash the blood away and then reported him to the captain for dirtying the holystone. McDonough also said that Colville flogged men with no provocation, and he alluded to 'other grievances too numerous to mention'.

The admiral promptly sent two captains from other ships to enquire into the case. As usual, they could find no sailor stupid enough to confirm the charges in front of Colville. Accordingly, they cleared the lieutenant.

Colville used the direct method to find out who wrote the letter. He assembled the ship's company and told them he would 'stop every indulgence it is in my power to give till I find the man or men who were concerned'.

McDonough had often kindly written letters home for men who could not write down their words themselves. These men did not come forward to name him. Even so his hand was well known, and several of the company appear to have named him. A funny thing happened on the way to the court martial.

The first witness was John Blake, the purser's steward. The prosecutor showed him the letter. Blake said the writing was like McDonough's hand in some characters, but different in others. William Colly, the captain of the forecastle, said that McDonough had indeed read him a copy of a letter. But it wasn't the same letter as the one produced in court. He thought the one he was looking at now was probably the work of James Martin. As it happened, Martin had recently run from the ship in Ireland and got clean away. Samuel Buckner, foremast man, did remember somebody saying, 'Shall we go down in the fore cock pit and write that now?' But he could no longer remember who had said those words. Thomas McSeed, master's mate, was called and sworn. He was asked one question: 'Do you know anything of your knowledge to prove that the prisoner wrote the letter you have read?' McSeed answered, 'I do not.'

Michael Divine, the captain of the foretop, had been in irons with McDonough off Belfast. He could not remember McDonough confessing anything to him then. He certainly had not had any conversation about a confession with George Hendrick. John Saunders couldn't remember anything. He especially did not remember telling the captain that many of the ship's company had known about the letter. John Burn, boatswain's mate, swore that the letter did not look like the prisoner's hand to him.

The final witness was George Hendrick, the boatswain's mate who hadn't had the conversation with Michael Divine. He knew nothing at all about the letter. He had never heard of it before the officers brought the matter up. The prisoner offered no defence and was acquitted.

This case shows the remarkable solidarity of the forecastle. It shows something else, too. The witnesses were not simple seamen. All but two were petty officers or 'captains', the men Colville had to rely on for daily discipline. On other ships such men were often witnesses for the prosecution.

Probably the Eurydices had been leaning on their petty officers. But both the petty officers and the big officers seem to have felt the men had a shadowy right to petition. The Navy and its courts could not approve of writing letters. Individual officers like Colville might be enraged, but in most cases, the authorities tolerated written complaints. In many cases they responded to them – after all, throughout history every despot has trumpeted the poor man's right of petition.

Letters were not completely innocent, though. There was always a veiled threat. After 1797 it was pretty much in the open. That year Black Dick Howe received many letters from different ships in the Channel Fleet asking for a pay increase. Black Dick, former admiral of the Channel Fleet, was relatively trusted. Some of the men clearly felt he would intercede for them.

Black Dick put the letters in his pocket. The subsequent mutinies shook the state and laid Ireland open to invasion. Howe had to do some embarrassed explaining in the House of Lords. After that, admirals were less likely simply to ignore letters.[7]

If the letter was the first resort of many a ship's company it was not the last. Sailors staged elaborate bits of theatre to make their point. William Richardson, for instance, was serving on the *Minerva* in 1793. The 19-year-old captain didn't like people talking on deck, and he hated swearing:

> Not an oath was allowed to be spoken, but as there were so many new pressed men in the ship it was almost impossible to avoid it, and when any was heard to swear their names were put on a list, and at seven next morning were punished, though not severely, few getting more than seven or eight lashes; yet it was galling, and how I escaped God only knows . . .

Though the punishment was light, it displeased the men very much, who had not had time to divest themselves of this new crime they had been so long accustomed to, and was nearly attended with serious consequence. Every evening, weather permitting, it was customary for the people to have a dance, and one of these evenings the lanthorns were lighted as usual, and hung on each side of the launch . . . and the fiddler on the topsail sheet bits began to play away on his violin; but nobody came to dance.

By-and-by the gunners' wads began to fly about in all directions, the lights were extinguished, the lanthorns knocked to pieces, and a wad rolled into the admiral's cabin as he walked there. The old boy soon saw that something was the matter and sent for Captain Whitby; but when Captain Whitby came he pretended that he knew nothing was the matter with the ship's company. The admiral's steward came into the cabin at the time, and being asked if he knew what was the matter with the people, replied that he heard the men say that there was too much dancing at the gangway in the morning to keep them dancing in the evening. [The men were flogged at the gangway.]

So the admiral, seeing through it immediately instead of using severe means (as many a tyrant would have done, and perhaps caused a real mutiny), adopted a better way, and that was in cautioning Captain Whitby not to use the cat on such light occasions, and never flog a man without his permission.[8]

The protest was carefully calculated. Dancing was a privilege, not a duty. It was supposed to be fun. The captain could not make them have fun without looking a fool. Moreover, they only threw the gunner's cloth wads. They could have used cannon balls.

On dark nights cranky sailors sometimes rolled cannon balls along the deck in the hope of breaking the legs of unpopular officers. The officers do not seem to have reported the matter. It must have been hard to identify the culprit in the dark. A report would also have exposed an officer's unpopularity to his superior. So most officers singled out for this treatment seem to have kept an ear cocked for the roll and jumped the balls as they came.

Richardson reports another inventive method of dealing with an awkward captain. In 1795 he was on the *Prompte*. The Promptes were never given shore liberty, so many ran. The embarrassed captain ordered a tight watch at night to make sure no potential deserters were on the move.

> So strict a guard was kept at night that a man could not go to the head [the toilet] without being challenged by the sentries with 'who comes there?' . . . so one day, when the captain went on shore, the girls of the town had made up their minds to have a little fun on the occasion with him, and when he came near they ranged themselves into a line, and one of them cries out 'who comes there?' another replies 'William Taylor' (the captain's name): 'Pass him along,' says another, and then they set up a hearty laugh, which so humbled him that there was no more 'passing' the people to the head of the ship afterwards.[9]

On other days the 'girls of the town' were to be found on board the *Prompte* as the 'wives' of the sailors; on land, though, there was nothing Captain Taylor could do to them.

Sometimes only mute protest was possible. During the war of 1812 Samuel Leech deserted from the British Navy to the American Navy, which had been modelled on British lines. Leech did not have to deal with the confusion of new ways. On the *Boxer* one of Leech's shipmates was trying to pilot the ship. He ran aground, doing the ship no harm:

> The captain flew into a passion, ordered him to the gangway, and commanded the boatswain's mate to lay on with his rope's-end. I did not witness the flogging, for the hands were not called up to witness punishment, unless administered by the cat-o'-nine-tails, but one of my messmates said that he received at least a hundred lashes. I saw him several days afterwards, with his back looking as if it had been roasted, and he unable to stand upright. He wore the same shirt in which he was flogged for some time afterward. It was torn to rags, and showed the state of his back beneath. His object in wearing it was to mortify and shame the captain for his brutality.[10]

On Christmas Eve 1802 the West Indian fleet was electric. The war was coming to an end. (It would begin within the year, but the politicians were not mentioning that yet.) While the sailors longed for home, on the islands the slaves longed for freedom. Some islands were in revolt. On others defeated movements remembered and waited. On San Domingo the slaves were in charge. Somebody would have to stay as minders for the planters.

The commodore decided the fleet would sail for England, with the exception of the *Excellent*. He also transferred three of the Excellents to the *Castor* so they could go home.

This favouritism was the last straw.[11] The master's log tells us what happened on Christmas Eve: 'In turning the hands up, found the ship's company aft in a body. On orders being given for their going to their duty they dispersed with evident remarks of discontent.' And that, the officers doubtless hoped, was that. At this stage nobody wanted to prosecute – they called it discontent, not mutiny.

After all, it was Christmas. The West Indian fleet was no place for whiners. But Christmas in a home port was usually one long party: unlimited drink, songs, fights, vomit and no discipline between decks. The custom was not observed on the *Excellent* this year although a certain rowdiness could be tolerated.

The commodore must have had other worries at the back of his mind. The *Excellent* had been sent out to keep an eye on the black revolutionaries in San Domingo.[12] The example could be contagious. After all, in these waters five years before the people had seized the *Hermione* and killed Captain Pigot. When the fleet returned to England, the *Excellent* would be vulnerable on her own, as the Hermione had been. The sailors on the ships returning to England would probably live. The majority of those who stayed would die, from disease. A sensible officer would hesitate before making enemies of his men in these circumstances.

On Christmas morning a stream of petty officers led small deputations to the quarterdeck. On many ships the petty officers took the men's grievances to the captain. On other ships the 'captains' of the tops and the deck stations took this role. It was an important line of communication. The petty officers and 'captains' were usually old and respected seamen. They were part of the forecastle world, but also agents of the captain's discipline. They were expected to approach the captain respectfully, their hats in their hands.

Not all captains encouraged this custom. On some ships the men must have felt it was a waste of time to talk to the captain. But all ships knew of the practice. At courts martial the judges sometimes told seamen they should have gone to their officers in this proper and respectful manner.

On the *Excellent* things were not that simple. Boatswain's mate Matt Loyal led a deputation on to the quarterdeck. When the commodore asked who had sent him there, Loyal replied 'that the ship's company had to know why they could not go home with the *Castor*. And that the men were grumbling about their wives [and] children, and that he had an old mother who had not seen him for eight years. He said that when the *Castor* got under weigh the ship's company meant to follow in the *Excellent* and see if it was a war or not.' (He meant that they wanted to check the rumour that peace had been declared.)

Loyal led his deputation off the quarterdeck. The commodore called him back on his own and said: 'Take care, you are speaking a little too fast.' The officers were still treating the events as petitions from the petty officers. But they were getting rattled.

The people went below for their dinner. Loyal reported to them; he told them not to send him aft again. He had been at sea many years, he said, and well understood the difference between home and abroad, but he could do no more. If they wanted to talk to the commodore, they could go themselves.

Those may not have been Matt Loyal's exact words. I have taken the speech from his evidence at the court martial, where he was fighting for his life. But there are two ways of reading that speech.

The men immediately gave three cheers and shouted,

'Home, home.' Sailors sometimes gave three cheers for the admiral. They usually gave three cheers as they headed into battle. The great Spithead mutiny had started with three cheers from the rigging of the flagship.

According to the log,

> hearing the Ships Co. Cheer on the lower deck the marines rushed on deck and the officers of the ship, and armed with all possible dispatch. The commodore . . . and a guard of marines and other officers went on the lower deck and pulling out the chiefs of the disturbance, had them secured, and sent to the Blenheim. Having dispersed the people and made every regulation to prevent any other disturbance happening . . . Kept a guard under arms to go round the decks with their officers.

Matt Loyal and 22 other men were put in irons and tried for mutiny. Subsequently, 13 were acquitted: one quartermaster, eight able seamen and two ordinary seamen. Ten men were convicted. One was sentenced to 200 lashes, four to 500 lashes each, and one man to 800 lashes. All six were seamen. Four petty officers were sentenced to death: a quartermaster, a quarter gunner, Loyal and Crabb, another boatswain's mate.

The officers did not bother to wait for the usual appeal to the Admiralty. The next day the four petty officers were hung in front of the fleet. At the same time all the convicted seamen were pardoned as a sign of the commodore's humanity.

At their trial Loyal and Crabb had argued that the petty officers were only doing their duty in representing the men to the officers. I can't tell if this was an honest defense by Loyal, though Crabb certainly organized protest. What is clear is that the Excellents were using customary forms of protest which suddenly turned into 'mutiny'.

These customary protests were not formal rituals where everybody knew what would happen next. Life on ship was potentially explosive. The men were very angry and heavily outnumbered the officers. The ships themselves were isolated and usually too dispersed for there to be an immediate source of reinforcements for the officers. The hierarchy of command was therefore tightly organized, constantly vigilant, obsessively violent. There were arms chests everywhere. Both sides remembered victorious mutinies and savage courts-martial. Any protest could shift abruptly into armed mutiny. Any collective complaint could be answered by an orgy of hangings. Once the people started murmuring and gathering in small groups, nobody knew what could happen next. This uncertainty explains a lot of the moderation and caution both sides showed in most confrontations.

# 4

## 'The footballs and shuttlecocks of a set of tyrants'

The press gathered in resentful men from every port in the Mediterranean and Atlantic. Bullying and corruption enraged them. They fought back. None of this was new but after 1789 the meaning of protest changed. The possible consequences of resistance were suddenly without limit. This was the age of the French Revolution.

The Scottish lawyer Cockburn remembered that time: 'Everything rung, and was connected with the Revolution in France . . . Everything, not this or that thing, but literally everything, was soaked in this one event.' William Wordsworth looked back to that time with fond nostalgia 'Bliss was it in that dawn to be alive, but to be young was very heaven.'[1]

From Boston to Istanbul the minority who read newspapers carefully followed every twist and turn in the Revolution. Tom Paine popularized the revolutionary message in his book *The Rights of Man*. In England and Scotland alone it sold 200,000 copies in a population of ten million. Hundreds of thousands more borrowed copies or listened as others read to them.[2]

Most people in Europe and its colonies might know little of the Declaration of the Rights of Man. But everybody knew that the people of Paris had destroyed the Bastille and cut off the king's head. These two events reverberated around the world.

They carried a symbolism everybody could understand. The state at this time was still in its purest form: a body of armed men. It was the soldiers drawn up before the crowd, their muskets levelled. It was the whipping at the crossroads and the hanging judge. At its centre was the political prison. The Tower of London had housed Mary Queen of Scots and a thousand other political prisoners. Now the Pitt regime sent London's democrats to the Tower. Enslaved Africans and press-ganged Irishmen, too, knew the meaning of the sack of the Bastille.

In 1792 the French beheaded their king. After that there was no going back. The king was head of state. He was also the first in rank in the world of a thousand ranks and orders. When Louis lost his head, the world of aristocracy lost its heart. In many different places people so long accustomed to the boot on their faces understood that the French were avenging themselves upon king and lords.

Paris was the capital city of one of the two great empires of the world. The king of France was the king of kings, the French aristocracy the most cultured and sophisticated ruling class in the world. Paris was the city of art and opera. France and Britain were the centre of the world system then, as Russia and the United States are now. Today people notice movements in Nicaragua and Poland; we would notice an armed workers' revolution in New York or Moscow far more. For our world, that would be the equivalent of what happened in Paris from 1789 to 1793. Great revolutionary movements are international: ideas do not stop for customs posts.

The French Revolution weakened the grip of both France and England on the world. 'Imperialism' has recently become a dirty word. At that time, however, the French and British Empires were both proud giants. Now, France looked inwards. England went to war with its rival in empire and the leading powers of Europe were swept into the conflict. The fortunes of war cut off client states and colonies from France and Britain. English agents fomented in the French Empire; French agents agitated among British slaves and Irish peasants. Many different sorts of oppressed people decided that their time had come.

San Domingo, the richest plantation in the Caribbean, was France's most important colony. On the stormy night of 22 August 1792 the leaders of the slaves of the north met to plan the rising. They were mostly African born, and their leader was a priest of the African religion named Boukman. They sacrificed a pig, shared its blood and then Boukman led them in prayer:

> The god who created the sun which gives us light,
> who rouses the waves and rules the storm, though
> hidden in the cloud, he watches us. He sees all that
> the white man does. The god of the white man
> inspires him with crime, but our god calls upon us to
> do good works. Our god who is good to us orders us
> to avenge our wrongs. He will direct our aims and
> aid us. Throw away the symbol of the god of the
> whites [the cross] who has so often caused us to
> weep, and listen to the voice of liberty, which speaks
> in the hearts of all.[3]

Boukman combined Africa and Paris, god and *liberty*.

That night the burning began, until every plantation in the northern plain was on fire. The revolution was to last for 13 years. Its leaders were slaves: Toussaint, a trusted steward on the plantation, and Dessalines, his back scarred for life by the whip. At the end both men were dead, Haiti was an independent country, and no Haitian would ever be enslaved again.

After 1792 there were insurrections of some sort on almost every island of any size in the West Indies.[4] On Grenada Jules Fedon, a free man of colour and himself the owner of slaves and a plantation, led the slaves and freedmen. They massacred the English planters and held almost all of the island from 1795 to 1797.

On St Vincent the rising was led by the tribal chief of the Black Caribs. These people were the descendants of the original Carib Indians and runaway slaves. They looked black, they spoke Carib and followed the customs of the Caribs. Three days after the news of the Grenada rising reached St Vincent, the Caribs joined the French whites. Together they wore the cockade of revolution and together they sacked the capital. The Caribs held out against the British army for 18 months. They kept their liberty. Today they live free in Central America.

In Europe, too, all manner of men and women looked to France. The Netherlands was an advanced country. The members of the democratic clubs were mostly men working at their trades, and the clubs were known as the 'Leather Apron'. They were at the heart of the revolution that, with French help, founded the Batavian Republic. In backward Transylvania the Vlach peasants sought the support of a high Austrian official in drawing up a petition in Latin to the local diet. In Germany philosophers and musicians, such as Hegel, Mozart and Beethoven, looked at Paris. In Hungary the peasants rose. In Naples many of the rank-and-file leaders of the democratic revolution were priests.[5]

In Belfast in 1791 the Society of United Irishmen was founded by a Protestant lawyer, an army officer and 12 wealthy Presbyterian merchants. Taking their inspiration from the French Revolution, these men looked to a united effort by both Protestants and Catholics to reform the Irish parliament. The United Irishmen quickly grew and enrolled humble folk. By 1795 they were seeking French help to overthrow the English; they had become republicans. By 1797 they were forging an alliance with the Defenders and the Whiteboys. The Defenders were a Catholic peasant organization that fought land wars with Protestant peasants; the Whiteboys maimed the cattle and attacked the persons of greedy landlords. In 1798 they rose together: Presbyterians, United Men, Defenders and Whiteboys.[6]

The Tree of Liberty was the symbol of the French Revolution. In 1792 crowds planted the liberty tree in the main square of many towns and villages throughout Scotland. In Lanark the provost reported 'an almost universal Spirit of Reform and opposition to the Established Government and Legal Administrators, which has wonderfully diffused through the manufacturing towns of this Country'.

Dundas was Britain's home secretary and Scotland's corrupt political boss. The people of Edinburgh celebrated the King's Birthday in June 1792 with three days of riot against Dundas. They pelted the soldiers with stones and dead cats. In court one rioter put forward the defence that the crowd had only been throwing dead cats at each other, and the soldiers had got in the way.[7]

In the same year nine London 'tradesmen, shopkeepers and mechanics' met in a pub to talk over the high cost of provisions. They formed a society to press for the vote for every sane male person. As political parties were illegal, they called their organization the 'London Corresponding Society'. The membership grew quickly. Like the Dutch democratic club, most rank-and-file members were workers.

By 1795 the society could hold a public meeting in Islington attended by 200,000 of London's one million men, women and children. Three days later a crowd the same size surrounded the King as he rode through the streets to open Parliament. They shouted: 'No War! No King! No Pitt! Peace!' They broke the window of the king's coach, but let him go.[8]

Many sailors were revolutionaries. In the 1790s the Irish courts sent thousands of convicted revolutionaries into the fleet. Many of them must have joined their less political fellows in deserting as fast as possible. Others must have fallen overboard or died of yellowjack. Nevertheless, at any one time after 1795 there were probably at least 2,000 Irish revolutionaries in the fleet. Some will have given up the fight but many must have watched and waited. Almost every ship probably had at least one active revolutionary like Lawrence Cronin on the *Hermione*. In 1798 the United Irishmen had branches on several ships: 28 men belonged to the branch on the *Defiance* alone. Valentine Joyce was both a United Irishman and the leader of the great mutiny at Spithead. There his cool political head made the difference between victory and defeat.

Working beside these political prisoners were many thousands more who had joined strikes, demonstrations and revolts on land. Between a quarter and a third of the sailors were Irish; quite a few were black. Those sailors who had not joined unrest ashore must have heard about it from those who had.

Sailors, moreover, were men of the world. They *travelled*. They came from ports and fishing villages with their backs to the land and their faces to the sea. By 1800 a solid minority of sailors had helped to put down slave risings. In these years all sailors knew that strikes and armed revolts were a possibility for men like them.

The ideas of the French revolution crop up everywhere. But they are subtly changed into words that fit the reality of class struggle on shipboard. Listen to Leech, for instance:

> The difficulty with naval officers is, that they do not treat with a sailor as a *man*. They know what is fitting between each other as officers; but they treat their crews on another principle; they are apt to look on them as pieces of a living mechanism, born to serve, to obey their orders, and administer to their wishes without complaint. This is alike a bad morality and a bad philosophy. There is often more real manhood in the forecastle than in the wardroom . . . It is needless to tell of the intellectual degradation of the mass of seamen. 'A man's a man for a' that'.[9]

Again, Richardson's ship captured a privateer in 1796: 'her crew were a complete set of democrats, who could not suppress their indignation at seeing the officers' servant doing any menial office for them, they said, "Why did not the officers do it themselves?" '[10]

In 1797 the fleet in the Thames joined the great strike over pay. They addressed a leaflet to their countrymen on land:

> Shall we who have endured the toils of a tedious, disgraceful war, be the victims of tyranny and oppression which vile, gilded, pampered knaves, wallowing in the lap of luxury, choose to load us with? Shall we, who amid the rage of the tempest and the war of jarring elements, undaunted climb the unsteady cordage and totter on the top-mast's dreadful height, suffer ourselves to be treated worse

than the dogs of London Streets? Shall we, who in the battle's sanguinary rage, confound, terrify and subdue your proudest foe, guard your coasts from invasion, your children from slaughter, and your lands from pillage – be the footballs and shuttlecocks of a set of tyrants who derive from us alone their honours, their titles and their fortunes? No, the Age of Reason has at length evolved. Long have we been endeavouring to find ourselves men. We now find ourselves so. We will be treated as such.'

The man who wrote that leaflet was a child of the French Revolution. But his words also echo years of struggle by men and women far removed from the Age of Reason.

For instance, in the great slaving part of Liverpool in 1775 there was a dramatic fall in trade. The sailors waited uneasily for the masters to try to force down wages. On one ship the rate for a voyage to Africa was cut from 30 shillings to 20. The seamen took down the rigging so the ship could not sail. Nine of them were promptly arrested. That evening a crowd of 3,000 sailors and women released them from jail.

That was Friday. On Monday morning flying pickets went from ship to ship. Thomas Crockett of the *Betsy* remembered that 'a great number of sailors, about 150 in number, armed with sticks and larger clubs were coming around the said docks boarding all the vessels therein and taking out all the people they found at work and board'.[12]

The strike was organized by a committee of nine sailors. Two men emerged as leaders: Jemmy Askew and a Mr H. Blow. Every morning the pickets met at the docks to get instructions.

Tuesday morning a crowd of sailors and women

demonstrated outside the Exchange, the business centre for the local merchants. Since the merchants ran Liverpool, it was also the town hall. The merchants hired and armed 300 men to quell the rising. That night the thugs fired on the crowd, killing several sailors.

Next morning, Wednesday, 1,000 sailors put red ribbons in their hats and 'broke open the dockside warehouses and the gunsmith's shop for arms and ammunition, and marched on the Exchange'. The subsequent indictment said they were armed with 'cannons, guns, musketts, musquetoons, blunderbusses, pistols, swords, cutlasses, knives, clubs, sticks, stones, bricks, and other offensive weapons'. [13] They set up their six cannon and began a methodical bombardment of the Exchange which lasted all day. Above their guns they flew the red flag. They also marched to the homes of prominent slaving employers, took all their possessions into the street and burnt them.

The merchants got the message. They sent desperate requests for reinforcements to the dragoons in Manchester. At the same time they negotiated with the sailors. The next afternoon the cavalry rode into town and arrested about 50 'ringleaders'. One of them was a woman later charged with inciting the men to fire on the Liverpool jail. Although rarely charged in court women were always to the fore in English and Scottish demonstrations and street fighting. The macho proprieties of the judges made them reluctant to try women.

Only eight ringleaders were convicted. They were sent into the Navy as punishment, not killed. It appears that the negotiations had produced an agreement to hold wages firm and punish rioters lightly.[14]

It was no accident that slaves were at the heart of the Liverpool riots. In the twentieth century the industrial economy has been centred on the internal combustion engine. The key industries – and the most militant – have been those based around it: coal, steel, power, rubber, auto, aircraft. In the eighteenth century the ship was central to the imperial economy. Ships carried coal, slaves, sugar, rum, cotton and cloth. So the militants were the slaves, the miners, the coal-heavers, the shipwrights, the dockers, the cloth-workers, the shoreside quarrymen, the smugglers, and the sailors.[15]

Many of these people drank in the same pubs as sailors. Out-of-work sailors might turn to quarrying or dock work. In the winter Cornish smugglers and fishermen went inland to work in the tin mines. In Dorset sailors hid from the press gangs in the Portland stone quarries. The quarrymen beat the daylights out of any press gang who wandered into their place of work. In Liverpool the men and women in other trades joined the sailors in 1775. In 1791 the sailors and shipwrights of Liverpool struck together for six weeks. In London sailors scabbed on the coal-heavers in 1776, but sailors were in the front row of London mobs.[16]

The Liverpool riots were unusually violent. In other ways, however, they were typical strikers of the time. Although trade unionism was no crime before 1795, it might as well have been: the courts and the blacklist ruled out formal organization on a national scale. Even so in each town and port the workers in a particular trade had customary wage rates and customary working rules. When they thought the local masters were trying something on, they came out on strike. There were no police and the authorities would send for soldiers from another town. While this was happening the strikers had to establish their position quickly. So they picketed out other workers and demonstrated boisterously in the town. Many of them lived hand to mouth and could not afford a long strike. The aim was to force the masters to negotiate immediately and make sure they thought twice before trying it on again. The historian Eric Hobsbawm has called these struggles 'collective bargaining by riot'.[17]

In 1792 a sailors' strike started in Bristol. From there it spread to ports all over England and Scotland. These strikes combined the old tradition of pay strikes with the new spirit of revolution. From Newcastle one employer wrote to the prime minister:

> When I look round and see this country covered with thousands of Pittmen, Keelmen, Waggonmen and other labouring men, hardy fellows strongly impressed with the new doctrine of equality, and at present composed of such combustible material that the least spark will set them ablaze, I cannot help thinking the supineness of the Magistrates very reprehensible . . . P.S. Shocking to relate, the mob at this moment are driving some seamen or officers that have discovered a reluctance to comply with their mode of proceedings naked through the town before them.[18]

The magistrates were not the only supine authorities. The local army and Navy officers did not dare take on the sailors either – nobody knew what the consequences would be. The strike was relatively peaceful *because* the sailors were so strong and confident.[19]

The port of Aberdeen shows how politics and strikes combined. In June of 1792 the people burned boss Dundas in effigy. In December they planted a tree of liberty in the main square. The authorities uprooted it. A few days later they descended on the harbour and stripped the rigging from the ships. They joined the movement for higher wages and set watches to make sure nobody scabbed. The lord provost had no idea that the organization of the sailors was 'so extensive in its numbers or so formidable for the Method, regularity and resolution of the actors'. The masters agreed to arbitration and the sailors seem to have won.[20]

The Navy had its own tradition of protest. In March 1783 the crews in Spithead 'insisted on being instantly paid their wages, and discharged from the navy, otherwise they were determined to run their ships ashore and destroy them'. When they were paid, several ships' companies came ashore together, 'With colours flying and bands playing, and all was complete harmony. Another group, however, determined to express their hatred of the midshipmen, dressed up a boy in the uniform of a midshipman and compelled him to clean the shoes of anyone they met in the streets: in front of the same group, to make a further point, marched a petty officer "greedily gnawing on a bone with little or no meat on it".'[21]

Across the channel the French sailors welcomed the revolution. By law all their officers were men of aristocratic blood. Now all France was rising against aristocrats. In the second half of 1789 there was a wave of riots in every port. From 1790 on there were mutinies on most ships in the French Navy. Officers were beaten up in the streets, thrown into prison and led to the guillotine. Work discipline broke down, and the sailors refused sailing orders. By 1793 three-quarters of the officers had left the fleet. At one point that year the Channel Fleet in Brest was under the control of a committee composed of one officer and one sailor from each ship.[22]

British sailors could easily keep in touch with events in France. In 1793 the city of Toulon went over to the British, taking with it a third of the French Navy. Difficult as it is to believe in our brutal time, throughout the war neither navy attacked fishermen. British and French fishing boats criss-crossed the channel as they had always done. Smugglers ran back and forth from Normandy to Cornwall. American merchant ships would run to France on one voyage and England the next. They passed around the news in public houses and taverns.

Take the example of Mary Anne Talbot. Talbot was the youngest of 16 illegitimate children of Baron William Talbot and a working class woman. Deserted by her father and orphaned by her mother, she was 'depraved' at the age of 13 by an officer of the dragoons. In his company she shipped for Santo Domingo as a drummer boy in 1792. They were re-routed to France. After her lover was killed in battle there, she deserted and walked across France to Luxembourg. There she took ship on a French privateer. Captured by the Royal Navy, she served as powder monkey at the 'Glorious First of June'. Transferred to a bomb vessel, she was captured by the French and spent 18 months in a French prison. Released in an exchange of prisoners, she slipped away and shipped with an American merchantman to New York. On the return voyage they put in to London. Talbot was pressed by the Royal Navy during a night on the town in Wapping. Faced with the Royal Navy again, she broke down and admitted her sex. She was discharged in time to join in the great riot against George III outside Parliament.

Talbot was 16 when she finally left the Navy, carrying war wounds that would disable her until her death at thirty. Her travels seem incredible today. At the time, they were not unusual for a sailor. Talbot was proud of her noble ancestry and remained a firm right-wing loyalist all her life. But many seamen learned something else from their travels.[23]

# 5

## 'I will blow them to the bounds of buggery before we come up without honourable terms'

On 9 November 1794 Thomas Troubridge took over command of HMS *Culloden*. Troubridge knew the ship was 11 years old and 'crank': it did not sail well. But the *Culloden* was a 74-gun line-of-battle ship, and Troubridge could count himself lucky to be in command.

A naval officer's career depended largely on who he knew. Promotion on merit alone was rare. Troubridge had no 'influence' and was fortunate to rise. His father was a baker in London's Strand. He must have been at least a small master baker to get his son accepted as an officer, and he may have been quite a respectable businessman. He wasn't rich, however, and other officers felt that Troubridge came from a humble home. In the words of the *Dictionary of Naval Biography*, Troubridge had to be 'the architect of his own destiny'.[1]

His previous command had been the frigate *Castor*. In May Troubridge and the *Castor* had escorted a convoy of merchantmen out of Jersey. They soon ran into several French warships. Troubridge had to strike his flag. A few days after his surrender he was present at the first major naval engagement of the war, the 'Glorious First of June'. Unlike the other ambitious captains in the British fleet, Troubridge was locked in the boatswain's store room of the French flagship. He spent the battle cursing the guard at the door,[2]

The British captured the French flagship and Troubridge, who immediately faced a court martial for the loss of the *Castor*. The Navy always tried the officers and men after a ship was lost. This was by no means a formality: many officers were broken in rank and some 'dismissed the service'. But Troubridge emerged from the trial with flying colours. The court raced through the business, cleared him of any blame and commended him for his actions.[3]

Troubridge was stuck ashore on half pay. As is the way with these things, half pay was much less than one-half of full pay. It didn't compensate for the many fiddles and skims a captain on active service had open to him. But more important, Troubridge was an ambitious man who had spent the last 20 years climbing the ladder rung by slow rung. Now war gave captains an opportunity to display their courage and merit. Troubridge could not be sure that peace would not break out the next year. He must have chafed at the bit. After four months he was given command of the *Culloden*.

He was in trouble almost immediately. Tuesday 18 November was a stormy night. The *Culloden* was moored at single anchor at St Helens, down the coast from Spithead. At one in the morning the ship ran aground abaft. Troubridge quickly ordered the guns moved forward to raise the stern and free the ship. The ship's company went into the hold to break open the water casks. Then they pumped the water out to lighten the ship. Within an hour the ship 'struck very heavy'. The rudder was knocked off. Troubridge was forced to run up a distress signal. No help came. The other ships in the small fleet were fighting the gale too, and one of them had also run aground.

All that day the gale continued. The pumps were manned constantly. The men threw provisions overboard to lighten the ship. Thursday they were still aground and still pumping. Troubridge ordered the men to jettison two and a half tons of shot. The Admiralty normally enquired closely after the fate of every missing cask and the gunner had to account for every cannon ball. Troubridge was clearly worried.

Friday the men were still pumping and throwing casks overboard. Saturday afternoon they finally got the ship off, with the loose rudder lashed to the side. The *Culloden* couldn't make it back to Spithead without a rudder and had to be towed in by the frigate *Fox*: Troubridge and his shame passed before the watchful eyes of the fleet.[4]

The Admiralty demanded a written explanation of the captain's reasons for anchoring in such shallow water. Troubridge's reply was defensive, almost desperate in tone. There was a heavy sea and a very low ebb tide.

> I believe so much sea has not been seen for many
> years . . . I imagine the place the Ship struck on was
> a Knowl, I have not had time to sound since . . . it
> appears from the unevenness of the ground that the
> Chart now published is erroneous with respect to
> soundings, if ships were to lay at St. Helens in
> common with S.E. Gales, I have no doubt but that
> accidents would frequently happen.

He added that other captains took the same risks, and the anchor had probably moved a little.[5]

There was something in what Troubridge said. However, naval ships had been anchoring safely at St Helens for centuries. In addition his admiral had already complained to their lordships in London that 'if the ships had considered themselves to be obedient of my motions those accidents would not have befallen them'.[6]

Troubridge may not have known about the knife in his back. He did know he couldn't afford to lose a second ship. He couldn't even risk an extensive refit. That in itself would probably mean a court martial. Even an acquittal there would leave a sadly blemished record.

So Troubridge kept reassuring the Admiralty that nothing was really wrong. Repairs could be done quickly and easily. The rudder might have been damaged, but the gudgeon pins that supported it were all right. Eight days after running aground, Troubridge was able to assure their lordships in London that he would 'be ready by Saturday for sea every exertion in my power their Lordship may depend on.'[7]

Of course he meant the exertions of the crew. But the people of the *Culloden* saw things differently. Selfish to the core, they cared less for their captain's career than they did for the lives of the 500 men on board. They all felt that the ship needed an extensive refit or she would sink next time the crew put to sea.

The Cullodens had been in the thick of the fight at the 'Glorious First of June' five months before. The ship had been badly hurt then, and unable to sail without help for some days. In the battle two of the Cullodens had been killed.

The previous year the *Culloden* had gone on a cruise to the West Indies. On the voyage out John Pope and John Williamson had fallen overboard and were drowned; Daniel Driscoll had died of illness and another man, John Peters, had drowned. In the West Indies John Tottle and James Watts had died of illness, Rees Watkins had fallen from the foretop to his death, and George Grubb and John Knight drowned. The ship sailed for England on 1 August. In the middle of September sick men began dying : William Pasco went on the fifteenth, and John Harris on the seventeenth. Thomas Search died on the nineteenth, and the captain's clerk five days later. Within a week a further five men died; Richard Batten, John Coombe, Henry Collins, John Ward and Abraham Dyke.

On 30 September the *Culloden* reached England and fresh provisions. The ship fell upon a convoy and impressed many of its seamen to make up the numbers. One hundred and twenty two men lay sick in the hold, the majority with fevers or the 'flux'. Ten had ulcers. Others had contusions, rheumatism, consumption, gravel, while Pat Ryan had a shrivelled testicle.[8]

The Cullodens' experience was not unusual. The war against France lasted from 1793 to 1815. In the 14 major battles of the war the Royal Navy lost 1,875 dead. More than 72,000 died from illness and accident; 13,600 were lost in ships that went down.[9]

This goes a long way towards explaining something which at first sight appears contradictory. The sailors were often mutinous and many were infected with the new doctrine of equality. Yet everybody who served in the Royal Navy was impressed by the enthusiasm and heroism Jack Tar showed in battle.

Jack Nastyface, for instance, hated the Navy and hated the officers. He also fought at Trafalgar. He idolized Nelson:

From the zeal which animated every man in the fleet,
the bosom of every inhabitant of England would
have glowed with patriotic pride . . . Men from the
ships that bore the brunt of the fighting would meet
on shore. They would say, 'Oh, you belong to one of
the *Boxing Twelves*, come and have some black strap

and Malaga wine,' at the same time giving them a hearty shake by the hand.[10]

Sailors were proud and patriotic. But this did not mean they were blood-thirsty. Sir William Dillon, for instance, was a patriot, a snob, and a flogger of the old school. He first saw battle as a midshipman at the 'Glorious First of June'. Afterwards the crew had to clear the decks: 'The number of men thrown overboard that were killed, without ceremony, and the sad wrecks around us taught those who, like myself, had not before witnessed similar scenes that War was the greatest scourge of mankind.'[11]

The sailors had contradictory feelings. Leech fought on HMS *Macedonian* in 1812 against the USS *United States*. The American ship won, and Leech deserted to the Americans. He married a nice woman from Connecticut, and 30 years later he tried to explain his feelings in the battle to an American audience:

Such was the terrible scene, amid which we kept on our shouting and firing. Our men fought like tigers . . . I felt pretty much as I suppose every one does at such a time. That men are without thought when they stand among the dying and the dead, is too absurd to be entertained a moment . . . Still, what could we do but keep up a semblance, at least, of animation? To run from our quarters would have been certain death from the hands of our own officers; to give way to gloom, or to show fear, would do no good, and might brand us with the name of cowards, and ensure certain defeat. Our only true philosophy, therefore, was to make the best of our situation, by fighting bravely and cheerfully. I thought a great deal, however, of the other world;

every groan, every falling man, told me that the next instant I might be before the judge of all the earth. For this, I felt unprepared; but being without any particular knowledge of religious truth, I satisfied myself by repeating again and again the Lord's prayer, and promising that if spared I would be more attentive to religious duties than before. This promise I had no doubt, at the time, of keeping.[12]

At Trafalgar Nastyface and the Boxing Twelves were on the winning side. Leech's captain ran up a massive 'butcher's bill' before accepting the humiliation of being the first British captain to strike to the Americans. Leech's pacifism may have had something to do with this experience. Both Nastyface and Leech were radicals and both deserters; yet they fought as patriots.

It takes a leap of the imagination to understand their attitude towards war. In our time the horror of war is at its worst on the battlefield and under the bombs. In their time it was at its worst in camp and on shipboard. Now officers who want to defend war feel they have to underplay the slaughter. Then Dillon, Nastyface and Leech all condemned the slaughter of battle. But Dillon liked the war and Leech and Nastyface hated it. Dillon liked the Navy; the two seamen hated it. Similarly, the democrats on shore staged massive demonstrations against the war. However, their slogans did not protest at the slaughter: they condemned the war taxes, the press gangs and the high cost of bread.[13]

For the sailors, the two worst horrors were the West Indies and a ship lost at sea. The Cullodens were lucky. They cruised to the West Indies, spent four months mainly sailing around, and returned. But among the soldiers who served on land the mortality from 'yellowjack' (yellow fever) was terrible. Many sailors, too regarded a long cruise in the West Indies as a death sentence. Samuel Richardson was a gunner. When he was sent to the West Indies his wife wanted to come with him. He tried hard to talk her out of it, but she insisted. Some of the crew were transferred to other ships. Most died. When the ship returned to England Richardson, his wife and two others were the only people left on board who had made the outward voyage.[14]

John Nicol went to the West Indies, too:

> While we lay at St. Kitts, I took the country fever, and was carried to the hospital, where I lay for some days; but my youth, and the kindness of my black nurse, triumphed over the terrible malady. When able to crawl about the hospital, where many came in sick one day, and were carried out the next to be buried, the thoughts of the neglect of my Maker, and the difference in the life I had for some time led from the manner in which I had been trained up in my youth, made me shudder . . . I could now see the land crabs running through the graves of two or three whom I had left stout and full of health. In the West Indies, the grave is dug no deeper than just to hold the body, the earth covering it only few inches, and all is soon consumed by the land-crabs.[15]

The fever spared many like Nicol. But when a ship went down most of the hands went with her. The *Royal George* capsized at Spithead in 1793 while being heeled over for cleaning. Most of her men and almost all of the 300 women on board drowned. The Navy discouraged its sailors from learning to swim, lest they desert. If the ship went down in the Atlantic or the North Sea, any who could swim froze to death soon enough. A large ship carried three boats: two large ones for the officers and one small one for the 500 sailors. As the ship went down the sailors swarmed up the rigging, fighting to keep above the waves. There was not yet among the officers the later custom that a captain should be the last to leave.

This was the fate the Cullodens feared. The surviving evidence shows that the *Culloden* was an old ship with weak masts and constant leaks. She sailed badly, particularly to windward. Indeed, Nelson thought Troubridge to be 'as full of resources as his old "Culloden" was full of defects'.[116]

The documentary evidence does not show if the *Culloden* was seaworthy after running aground. We do know that the Cullodens themselves were agreed that the ship was not fit to be taken out. Hundreds of them were willing to risk their lives to stop the ship sailing. Most of these men had sailed together for two years; about a third of them were skilled sailors bred to the sea. I think we can trust their judgement over Captain Troubridge's.

The people let the officers know they were upset. They began to murmur. 'Murmuring' was a common tactic. Small groups of men would gather and talk to each other by the lee rail. As an officer passed they became suddenly quiet. Raised voices drifted up from below through the fore hatch, but the words were indistinct. Subtle changes in look and manner made it clear the people were angry. Such signs also gave warning to the officers that the men might be contemplating further steps. So it was in the *Culloden*. In his defence at the court martial Francis Watts said, 'there were continued Murmurings in the Ship before the Mutiny.'

James Calloway was flogged the day after the ship returned to Spithead. He got 24 lashes for 'mutiny and contempt to a superior officer'.[7] The sentence was stiff, but not that unusual. The offence was unusual. 'Mutiny' could cover a multitude of virtues. It might mean getting drunk and cussing an officer. It sometimes meant planning an insurrection, but the penalty for that was more than two dozen lashes. It could mean refusing to do a job and shouting about it. At this time and place it probably means that Calloway had said something about the state of the ship and refused to withdraw it.

The men went beyond murmuring. At the trial Lieutenant Griffiths said that 'some day previous to the Fourth they refused to bring their hammocks up. When piped and on Captain Troubridge and the officers going below they called out a new Ship.' The day's work began with the men bringing their hammocks up to air. In effect, this was a lightning strike. On some ships such a demonstration would have been treated as mutiny. The Cullodens could have been tried and hanged. But Troubridge was in no position to face a court martial. He talked the men back to work.

This demonstration probably happened on Tuesday 2 December, two days before the mutiny. At the court martial Lieutenant Owen was asked, 'Had any complaint been made on the 2d. December after the ship had struck?' He answered, 'None had been made on 2d. December in a regular manner.' At court martial witnesses chose their words with great care. We can assume there was a complaint on that date in an irregular manner.

At some point in this week *some* of the Cullodens decided there was no real hope of moving Troubridge. They began to organize a mutiny. Probably they made the decision on Tuesday night following the hammocks protest. The ship was due to sail on Saturday 6 December. The murmuring continued. By Thursday night many people on both sides sensed that something was about to happen.

David Hyman collapsed into his hammock at seven o'clock that night. He was tired from a long day rowing the ship's launch into town and back. Hyman was a 22-year-old Irishman from Cork.[18] He was no sailor: he was still rated a landsman after two years in the ship. But the officers trusted him enough to put him in the crew of the launch, with all the opportunities for desertion that job offered.

Hyman couldn't sleep. At about eight Isaac Flinn was making a noise on the fore hatch gratings. Hyman 'desired him to make no more noise, as I was much fatigued, and on duty the most part of the day. On this the boatswain replied, "You are a very bad fellow, and what business have you here at this time?" '[19]

Soon after this Hyman fell asleep. He woke to find the master, John Murray, beating him about the face. Hyman said, 'What did you do that for?'

Murray told him it was because of the affair that was about to happen. Hyman told the master to go away. The master walked aft, slapping the men in their hammocks as he went. He was presumably trying to frighten them and defuse the threat of mutiny.

It didn't work. To quote Hyman, 'In a few minutes after, Lieutenant Owen and the ship's corporal came down the fore hatchway. And about as near as I can judge, about forty or fifty men, huzza'd forward in the bay, and a number of shot rolled aft along the deck.'

Some of the men called out to others to stand fast heaving the shot and hear what Owen had to say. He tried to 'reason with them'. With one voice they replied from the dark that the ship had struck and they would not go to sea. They demanded 'a new ship or this one overhauled'. Some moderate voices said they had no objection to their officers and were prepared to serve with them on another ship. Some militant voices added that if they went to sea they 'would not fire a shot, but would be taken by the French'. The men began throwing cannon balls at Owen in the dark, cramped space between decks. He fled back on deck.

The mutineers swept through the ship below decks. They were hunting for skulkers hidden behind the bulwarks and gentlemen cowering in their berths. Joseph Curtain was a 21-year-old landsman from Cork. He shouted that they must drive all the quartermasters and quartergunners on deck: 'We are not be hung on account of them.'

All over the ship men made split-second decisions. Loyalists leapt for the hatchway ladders. Most of them got up on deck. The people pulled the ladders down. Now waverers could not go up and the marines could not storm down. The people put sentries on each hatch. They surrounded the hatches with hammocks to conceal the identities of the activists below. They broke into the magazine and handed out muskets and cartridges. Armed sentries guarded every critical point below decks. Barricades went up in case the officers tried to come down again.

Samuel Triggs took charge of the guns. He was a 27-year-old Cornishman bred to the sea.[20] He had been in the ship just under two years, and had years as a seaman behind him. His officers had always regarded him as a 'diligent, sober, deserving man'. He'd had enough. He got a gang to manhandle two of the guns so they faced towards the hatchways the marines would have to come down. Triggs stood by one of the guns holding a lighted slow match. He was to remain there for the five days and nights of the mutiny.

Up on deck Troubridge began to count his forces. His clerk took down the name of every loyal man for future reference. Troubridge found he had the majority of his officers. But four petty officers and four midshipmen were still below. (They were cowering from the polite but firm mutineers.) Troubridge had all but six of the marines. He also had 13 seamen. Over 300 men remained below. They had the guns, the muskets, the ammunition, the food, the water and the initiative. Troubridge realized he had to negotiate.

He headed for the after hatchway to talk to the people. There was hubbub from the decks below. Some of the people threatened to shoot up the hatchway. Cornelius Sullivan kept poking his musket up through the hatch and threatening to shoot Troubridge. Sullivan was a 22-year-old landsman from Bandon in Ireland. He was angry, and unlike most of the mutineers he was drunk. The people shouted up the hatchway their demand for a new ship. One voice added that bringing three or four other ships alongside would not make them give up their purpose. Sullivan remembered an insult from First Lieutenant Whitter. He jeered up at Troubridge, 'Where is Whitter with his empty pistols now? Why does he not come down and frighten us now?'

Troubridge retreated from the hatchway and sent off a letter to the admiral. Below decks the men consolidated their organization. Francis Watts had been a leader from the beginning. He was only 21. Like all the others leaders we know of, he had joined the *Culloden* early in 1793. He had been to the West Indies and back and fought at the 'Glorious First of June'. He was no sailor. He was rated a landsman. His station was in the afterguard, a largely unskilled job pulling on ropes. Much of the time, however, he actually did duty as a tailor.

Watts was born in Launceston in the centre of the Cornish tin-mines: union country. He probably did not join the Navy from Cornwall, for Launceston is too far from the sea and the press gangs were scared of the militant Cornish. He might have joined from London, where trade unionism was strong among tailors.[21]

Wherever he had been pressed, Watts was certainly a worker and an organizer. On shore many such craftsmen were self-taught intellectuals, though Watts himself was not. Unable to read, he had to go in search of somebody to write out watch bills for him.

Seaman John Walker agreed to do it. Watts wanted the men divided into nine watches. Walker listed 27 men in each watch. In all, 243 were 'watched'. Each watch had a corporal who placed the men at their sentry stations. Each watch stood sentry for two hours in every 18.

The leading mutineers began to administer oaths to every man below, handing each in turn a big Bible. A silent crowd surrounded the two. If a man showed any hesitation the crowd shouted for him to kiss the book and swear.

We don't know the exact wording of the oath. People took oaths seriously then. At the subsequent court martial prosecution witnesses whose evidence helped to hang their shipmates refused to repeat the oath they had taken. They would only say that the general meaning was that they would reveal nothing to the officers afterwards. Some witnesses added that they would not surrender until they had a new ship.

Every man below was sworn. The officers were not sworn, but confined to a cabin so they could not see what was going on. Similarly, it looks as if the women were not sworn. In all the court martial evidence women are never referred to, though this does not mean that none were present. Everybody knew that women were *never* called as witnesses at a court martial.

Everything points to careful organization before the

mutiny and tight discipline during it: the way potential scabs were driven on deck, the hatches stripped of ladders, barricades built and the magazine broken open, and the way men were watched and sworn. One thing above all else points to careful discipline. As on any evening, several men were drunk at the beginning of the mutiny. The mutineers had broken into the magazine at the first opportunity. Between them and the spirit room was one paltry lock, which they could have broken with ease. Nobody touched it: Three hundred thirsty tars went cold sober for five days and nights.

Who planned and led the mutiny? This is not an easy question to answer. The Cullodens tried very hard to shield their leaders. Nevertheless, there are some pointers, and we shall return to them in the next chapter.

As the people were being sworn below, Troubridge was writing off to Admiral Lord Bridport, his immediate superior. By early morning the admiral despatched his fifth lieutenant, George Delanoe, to talk to the Cullodens and report back. The men allowed Delanoe below to negotiate directly with them. He told them he would represent their demands to the admiral and promised them a fair deal. They told him they wanted a new ship. Some men also shouted that they wanted rid of Lieutenant Whitter. Others shushed them, emphasizing that a new ship was their only demand.

Delanoe went back to Admiral Bridport, who in turn reported to Parker, the admiral in command on land in Portsmouth. Parker did not know what to do. The Cullodens were armed and prepared to fight. On the other hand, he didn't know how the Admiralty in London would react if he gave in and offered the men a complete refit for the *Culloden*. Parker decided to write to the lordships and to send Lord Bridport and two captains to talk to the Cullodens.

The three officers came on board on Saturday morning, 36 hours after the start of the mutiny. They spent their time 'expostulating and reasoning with a part of the crew . . . without being able to make any seeming impression of their determinations, which *All* on the Ship having been on shore, insisting on that Account of her being docked, or their removal to another ship'.[22]

The Cullodens decided to submit their case in writing. As letter-writer they chose James Johnston the Second, a 23-year-old landsman from Godalming in Surrey. (He was called 'the Second' to distinguish him from another Culloden, James Johnston the First.) His letter survives. The hand-writing is good and the style clear. He obviously had some education, but he was no gentleman:

> H.M.S. Culloden Saturday Morning
> My Lord,
>     I am desired and appointed by the Ship's
> Company to address your Lordship on a subject
> which is very disagreeable to me, and must certainly
> be to every individual concerned especially where the
> lives of so many Brave Sailors is at stake. Your
> Lordship seemed to approve of our former conduct
> and likewise was pleased to Compliment us thereon,
> and especially when we were most depended on, that
> was when we were to contend for the Honour of our
> King, Officers & Country we did it without the
> least reluctance and gladly embraced the favourable
> opportunity to distinguish our courage and valour, in
> so Glorious a Victory – we now ask your Lordship
> candidly to consult your feelings (as we know you

are possessed of the Nicest feelings possible can be inspired in the Breast of Man) and see if our case does not deserve to be Minutely and favourable looked into they therefore hope your Lordship will consider their State, as it seems rather precarious and as they seem to be all of one opinion that the Culloden is not fit for his Majesty's Service without being either overhauled or more properly examined and is surprised that any Ship Wright should report a Ship sound after so many and Violent Strokes as she received at different times especially when the damage lies so far under water, likewise thinks it is impossible to assertain the true State the Ship's bottom is in. There is another objection which seems rather displeasing that is the indifferent usage of our first Lieutenant Mr. Whitter – in the first place he as represented us as a set of Cowardly Rascalls, and that he was the person that should have cowed'd them with a small empty Pistol, which is enough to irritate the mildest and couldest tempers in Mankind in the next place his usage altogether is quite different from any we have hitherto received. They therefore hope your Lorship will take the trouble of Visiting us once more when we will be best able to Treat with your Lordship upon what terms we can most Amicable and Honourable Settle. be Pleased to favour us with the sight of their Lordship's letters from the board of Admiralty thats concerning the present Crissis.

I am my Lord your
very Humble and
Obedient Servant, A delegate.

Johnston wrote his letter as the usual respectful petition. He used the common politeness and soft soap. But behind the customary phrases, we can hear the people between decks feeling their power. The case is clearly and professionally stated. The sting comes in the last lines: 'to treat with your Lordship upon what terms we can most Amicable and Honourable Settle.' This is the language enemies and equals use for negotiation: 'treat . . . terms . . . settle'. And the men wish to settle with their honour intact. Honour was usually reserved to gentlemen. The mutineers did not believe that admirals necessarily possessed honour. That is why they ask to see the correspondence from the Admiralty. They imply that Lord Bridport might have been concealing the Admiralty's true intentions. As we shall see, he did.

The signature sums it up. Johnston is Lord Bridport's very humble and obedient servant. He is also 'a delegate'. The word comes from the French Revolution, and was used by British radicals and trade unionists. It means the democratically elected representative of a people in struggle.

The Cullodens were confident. Friday morning the moderates had shushed those who complained about Lieutenant Whitter. They probably wished to appear reasonable and stick to the important demand. By Saturday, however, the Whitter-haters had the upper hand. Johnston attacked him on behalf of the whole ship's company.

What did they have against Whitter? It's difficult to tell. The character of the first lieutenant was of enormous importance on any ship. Whitter had been a lieutenant on the *Culloden* since early 1793. But he had only been promoted to first lieutenant on 27 November 1794, right after the accident and a week before the mutiny. Until then the *Culloden* seems to have been a reasonably happy ship, as these things went. The Cullodens had known Whitter for some time. They probably watched his behaviour in his new job with nervous expectation.

This is what made the incident of the empty pistols so significant. We don't know if he actually fired an empty pistol in somebody's face. My guess is that he crowed over the men after the failure of the hammocks protest. Whatever he did, the people took it as a sign that he would not make a good shipmate.

There is a postscript to the letter. Johnston must have read out what he'd written to his mates, only to find that they wanted changes. The addition is in Johnston's hand, but the writing is shakier. He probably wrote it standing up:

> P.S. The Ship's Company surrendurs on the following propositions. Ist a new ship or the Old one Docked or all the people at present between decks [word unreadable here] on board of different ships as your Lordship think most proper & your Lordships word and honour not to punish any man concerned in the present business or to mention or remember it there after.

The letter combines tact and threat. The postscript is the blunt bottom line. Incredibly, it was signed by Johnston and William Leader. A third man's name is written and then crossed out so that it cannot be read. That was probably Watts: one witness said he had helped with the letter.

The letter was handed up the fore hatchway on the end of a cleft stick. It was taken by Fourth Lieutenant Digby Willoughby. He duly carried it to Captain Troubridge. The beleaguered captain carried it across to Lord Bridport and opened it in the admiral's presence. Even in a crisis, the admiral was sheltered from direct contact with the power of the people.

Admiral Bridport took the letter to Admiral Parker on shore. Parker reported to the Admiralty in London. Their lordships' response was coloured by what had just happened on the *Windsor Castle*.[23]

The *Windsor Castle* was a 98 gun line-of-battle ship. It was part of the Mediterranean fleet. On the evening of 9 November 1794 the hands were turned up. They refused duty and assembled on the lower deck 'in a most riotous and mutinous manner, pointing the foremost guns aft, seizing the small arms which were in the Gun Room, and firing several of them off, barring in the Ports fore and aft'.

The officers and marines attempted to force the lower gun deck. They failed. The captain came on board and led the marines below again. They failed. The lower gun deck was too well fortified. The people kept shouting for a new captain and a new lieutenant.

Next day the men wrote the admiral a letter:

Admiral Hotham
Sir
   Necessity has Obliged us to proceed to our present Oeconomy, which necessity is thus. Since Admiral Cosby Left us we have had a very Different Kind of Usage to that what we had at the time he was with us, for no man can go aloft now, But what he is in dread of being punished with Lashes, their wine is stopt and given to another part of the Ships Co. which is quite contrary to the rules of the Navy, and Yesterday Morning the scouring stone was not to be found, all the Main top Men was Called up to Know what was become of it, every man said he knew nothing of the matter, a Brick was immediately put in the hands of every man in the

ship (we were in three watches) and all hands of them was made to scour the 2nd and main deck, and last evening bricks were issued out again to the main top men, the first lieut., told them in a short time they should have a heavyer burden on their backs, two or three of them smiling together on a different affair, was pooped, and one seized up to mizzen riggen, them men that came on liberty from other ships, was called up and pooped for reasons we know not, which hurted us very much, and we never had the like usage before, we should have presented the case to Admiral Linzee before we had proceeded thus, but, we very seldom have the opportunity of seeing him and no petitions is admitted to him. for these reasons we desire other officers and better usage, for at present we are used in a cruel and oppressive manner, and we wish no more than to share a similar usage with the Britannian's ships company. (and the Boatswain to exchange duty, for we cannot live with his tyranny)

We hope your honour will take this into consideration, and mitigate the oppression of your most Obedient humble

Servants<br>Windsor Castles Ships Co.

The complaint about the boatswain is jammed in between the lines in small handwriting. It looks like an angry afterthought.

The letter reflects the 'moral economy' of the Windsor Castles: their outraged sense of traditional rights. Their 'usage' is not moral. Their wine is stopped 'quite contrary to the rules of the Navy'. On Sundays they had their one moment of permitted relaxation when they entertained men from other ships in the fleet. Their private space was violated and their guests punished. The shame 'hurted us very much'.

The maintopmen were clearly at the centre of it all. 'No man can go aloft now' and punishment of the topmen is constant. The first lieutenant could not find the scouring stone, the large block of stone used to scrape the decks during cleaning. His mind immediately flew to the possibility that the maintopmen had heaved it over the side. He was probably right. A scouring stone was far too big to lose. *Somebody* had deep-sixed it, and they meant to convey a message to the officers.

There was clearly a conflict between topmen and officers here. The root of it was conflict over work aloft and work cleaning. The maintopmen were the elite of the crew. They were mostly men bred to the sea and almost all able seamen. They were also often the informal leaders of the ship's company. This was no revolt of disgruntled quota men and politicized landsmen.

The most striking thing about the letter is the *tone*. It is polite, detailed, logical and firm. It does not plead, it is not defensive. There is no crawling. The letter is the work of men fully aware that they held the initiative.

The Mediterranean was largely enemy territory. The *Windsor Castle* had guns and the men were prepared to use them. The ship was more than a match for any single line-of-battle '74'. Moreover, the fleet could not afford to lose men and ships in a civil war.

The day after the letter, Admiral Linzee came on board. He attempted to 'bring them to a sense of thier duty,'[24] They wouldn't budge. So Captain John Shield and First Lieutenant George McKinley were rowed across to the *St*

*George*. There they faced a court martial.

This was quite extraordinary. At first glance the admiral seemed to be taking the men's side. Certainly, he was at least treating their complaints with the respect they deserved. However, this was not how the men saw it. The admiral sent a letter to the ship's company asking them to produce a list of witnesses against their officers. The people were assembled on deck. They replied that the paper they had submitted was all they had to say. They would produce no witnesses.[25]

One can perhaps surmise that the men felt that witnesses might be punished later. One might even venture to suggest that the whole thing was a judicial charade designed to break the mutiny. Nothing, of course, could be more foreign to the tradition of British justice. But it does appear the Windsor Castles entertained some such suspicion.

The court martial could only have confirmed their doubts. A string of officers from the *Windsor Castle* testified that they had never heard or seen anything but perfect behaviour of the most humane kind from the captain and first lieutenant. The court cleared them on the grounds that no witnesses had come forward to back up the charges. The court was careful not to say the charges were untrue. The captain and first lieutenant walked free.

In theory, they still commanded the *Windsor Castle*. In practice, the Windsor Castles commanded themselves. The morning of the court martial Captain Gore came on board and read an order from the admiral taking over acting command. Unimpressed, the crew remained on the lower gun deck. At six that evening the court martial gave its verdict. Nobody knew who was in charge. An hour later Admiral Linzee came up the side. He assembled the crew and gave them everything they were asking for. A new captain and a new first lieutenant read their commissions to all hands.[26]

Nobody was punished. Next day the ship's log recorded the crew 'drying sails and other jobs as the service required'. Mutiny worked. Armed and disciplined mutiny prevented victimization.

Thre are obvious similarities between the mutinies on the *Windsor Castle* and that on the *Culloden*, four weeks later. The Cullodens may or may not have known about the *Windsor Castle*. One ship had come to Portsmouth from the Mediterranean with a crew who knew the story, but they were still in quarantine.

The Admiralty on the other hand did know. The *Windsor Castle* was a precedent; giving an amnesty to the Cullodens would make it a habit. Without terror they would face a rash of mutinies. The Admiralty told Parker to give in to the Cullodens and send the ship to the Hamoaze for repairs. But he was not to promise an amnesty.[27]

Admiral Parker was caught in the middle. He dithered for two days. He sent Captain Pakenham to negotiate with the obstinate Cullodens. According to Pakenham, he persuaded the men that the ship was seaworthy. He pointed out that for some days the pumps had produced only black bilge-water: a sign that there was no longer a leak. The men saw the point of that. Nevertheless they refused to come up without an amnesty.[28]

At six in the morning on Tuesday 9 December Parker received a letter from the Admiralty. He was instructed to put two three-deckers alongside the *Culloden* and take the ship. Parker replied that the wind was blowing too hard at that moment for him to communicate with the ships off Spithead.[29]

Parker was stalling. On the second day of the mutiny Surgeon's Mate George Jarvis had gone below decks on the

*Culloden*. He was needed for a gravely ill man in the sick bay. Before he was taken down there the Cullodens swore him to silence. While he was below decks, however, he was taken aside by three of the loyalists trapped with the mutineers. They told him that some of the Cullodens were threatening to blow up the ship.

Jeremiah Collins was one of the loudest of the intransigents. He was an able seaman from Cork, and at the age of 40 had spent much of his life at sea. He had probably had enough. He told one man that 'he was the man who would blow the ship up with an Inch of Candle before they should get their ends'. This was not an idle threat. An inch of candle in the magazine would destroy the whole ship and everybody on board in seconds. He told another man, 'by the holy St. Jesus, before we will go up without coming to honourable terms I'll blow them to the bounds of buggery'.

Surgeon's Mate Jarvis realized that the men who were telling him this were very frightened. They were not a front for the mutineers – indeed, two of them later testified extensively for the prosecution. They wanted Jarvis to warn the officers when he went back on deck.

Admiral Parker could not know how seriously to take such a threat. But he did know it would be a great risk to try to take the *Culloden*. Nobody knew what would happen if seamen were sent to put down mutineers, because nobody had ever dared try it. It was quite possible that the men on the other ships would refuse to fight. Then Parker would be facing a mutiny by the whole fleet.

As soon as he could contact the fleet, Parker told the captains of the *Royal George* and the *Royal Sovereign* to prepare to take the *Culloden*. First, he would try one last stratagem. He sent Captain Pakenham to talk to the men again.[30]

Pakenham went aboard and talked to the men down the hatch. There is dispute about what he said. At the court martial one of the judges asked Pakenham if the men had proposed any conditions for their surrender. He replied, 'Yes, they desired to give my word and honour for pardon for them. But this I declined as did also Captain Troubridge, and indeed it was not thought of by us.'

This is not really believable. Pakenham and Troubridge *must* have at least thought of meeting the men's demands. Parker was under intense pressure from London; Troubridge was finished if they stormed the ship; Pakenham was the man of the moment. He must have been tempted to promise amnesty and betray later. The captain of the *Defiance* was to take this line in 1795. The Admiralty were to try it on at Spithead in 1797.[31] It could solve everything so neatly.

In later years the sailors of the fleet believed that Pakenham promised an amnesty.[32] We do not know if he did. There were whispers at the court martial: that is why Pakenham was asked about conditions. But how can we be sure? Unfortunately, the most pertinent document is missing. The Admiralty records contain a letter from Parker reporting on the end of the mutiny. Parker says that he encloses a report from Pakenham. The enclosure is missing.[33] Enclosures and letters are often missing from the Admiralty records. The other letters and enclosures about the *Culloden* in 1794, however, are all there. Perhaps the letter was destroyed. Perhaps a lord of the Admiralty borrowed it and forgot to return it.

In any case, we should not pay too much attention to the popular version of events. Any historian can tell you that such incidents are rapidly covered in legend and rumour. And if we believe the sailors, we have to disbelieve the word of honour of a British officer at a court martial, given after a full and binding oath with his hand on the Bible. One can only assume that in the stress of the moment the Cullodens suffered a mass auditory hallucination.

Pakenham finished speaking to the people. Below decks they discussed what to do. Samuel Triggs, the 'corporal of the gun', said, 'We better go on deck. If our muskets are fired we will all be hanged. The longer we stay the worse it will be for us.' The people decided to come up. They sprang for the hatchways. Pakenham gave a hand up to Francis Watts and called him a 'good fellow'. The ship's company fell in for muster.

The mutiny was over.

# 6

## 'The most active ringleaders and the most proper objects for a Court Martial'

Whatever Pakenham may have promised, Troubridge and his officers immediately began questioning the men. Next day Troubridge had ten men in irons. He sent them to another ship to await trial. He wrote to the admiral that they appeared 'to have been the most active ringleaders, + the most proper objects for a Court Martial'.[1]

Who planned and led the mutiny? Were these ten men really the leaders? Yes and no.

The ten defendants were the ten men Troubridge could find witnesses against. Two of them were drunk and noisy the first night of the mutiny, but not leaders. Two of them faced weak evidence and were acquitted. One had done nothing but stand sentry like 252 other men.

But five of the prisoners seem to have been leaders: Francis Watts, James Johnston, Jeremiah Collins, David Hyman and Samuel Triggs. And James Petery was named at the court martial as a 'corporal of the watch', though he did not stand trial. Petery was a 23-year-old Highlander from Inverness who entered the *Culloden* as an able seaman.

Three of these six leaders were English, two were Irish and one Scots. Three were landsmen and three able seamen. Their average median age was 23. The leadership were like the mutineers as a whole: a coalition of Irish and British, seamen and landsmen.

There were other leaders, too. We do not know the names of six of the nine 'corporals of the watch'. And remember that the mutiny began with a crowd of 50 or 60 men cheering and rushing forward. Who made up this hard core?

Troubridge thought he knew. On the third day of the mutiny he wrote to Bridport that 'the Mutineers appear to me about 50 or 60 and mostly of the lower order of Irish, I have the names of the most active and riotous among them'. He said the Irish 'over-awed' the others.[2] Troubridge was defensively trying to explain his failure. He must have been tempted to lay the blame on a minority of unwashed Irishmen, implying that he had not really lost the loyalty of the decent Englishmen. He would be neither the first nor the last man to use that excuse.

The day after the mutiny ended Troubridge wrote to the admiral that he had the names of 30 men who had played an important part in the affair. He wanted them off his ship. After the mutiny, they were transferred.[3]

These men were not necessarily the hard core. Indeed, the case against them was probably thin.[4] They *may* have been active in the mutiny. We know they had been marked down as trouble-makers before. Indeed, some gave evidence for the defence at the trial. All that is certain is that they were the sort of men Troubridge and his officers *thought* would lead a mutiny.

Of these 30 men 19 were Irish; one was Jamaican, probably black; one was a Scot; four were born in London, two in Worcester, and one each in Plymouth, Devon and Cornwall. Thirteen entered the *Culloden* as landsmen, eight as ordinary seamen, eight as able seamen, and one as a carpenter's mate.[5] Ten of them entered as Irish landsmen: perhaps 'Irishmen of the lower sort'. Despite Troubridge's claims, there are ten Britons and eight able seamen among these 30 hard cases. The average age was twenty-two and a half.

We can compare this hard core with a group of loyalists. At the start of the mutiny 13 sailors and all but four marines ran up to join the officers on deck. During the mutiny some of the more 'mischievous' mutineers took the clothing and bedding of these loyalists, which they cut up into little pieces. After the mutiny Troubridge asked the Admiralty to compensate the loyal sailors and marines for their losses. He itemized for each man under various headings: shirts, shoes, stockings, coats, waistcoats, breeches, hats, beds, blankets, handkerchiefs and jackets.[6]

From these lists we can identify the 13 loyal seamen. Four of these half-naked men were Irish, one Italian, two Scots, and six English. Four were landsmen, three ordinary seamen, and five able seamen. One was a boatswain's mate. The average age was twenty-three.

The loyalists were a bit more skilled than the hard core of mutineers. They were quite a bit more English. But both mutineers and loyalists contained a spread of nationalities and skills. The mutiny was not a revolt of Irishmen and landsmen led by political landsmen. It certainly included some of each group. Rather, the rebels and their leaders were a coalition of the different kinds of sailors – as were the trouserless ones.

The court martial convened on 15 December 1794, one week after the end of the mutiny. In accordance with the custom, Troubridge was prosecutor. Among the judges were Pakenham and two other officers, who had been on the *Culloden* at some point in the mutiny. The regulations stated that every captain or admiral in the port had to serve on the court, except the admiral in charge.

Troubridge had written that the ten prisoners were the 'most proper objects' for a trial. The word 'objects' was ominous. The eighteenth-century court martial was a show trial; it was several other things as well. The judges tried to retain a sense of justice. They had to.

For one thing, most courts martial had nothing to do with mutiny. The bread and butter of the courtroom were disputes between officers, failures by officers and offences by individual seamen.

Disputes between officers were common. Ships were small. Officers lived on top of each other. They had to eat three times a day with men they often hated. Often a man would take orders from his social inferior and this was a source of much friction. Fletcher Christian of the *Bounty* may have been rated as master's mate; but his uncle was a leading member of the House of Commons and his brother was Professor of Jurisprudence at Oxford. William Bligh may have been captain; he was also the son of a customs officer and had been promoted from the lower deck. We may be certain that neither Bligh nor Christian ever forgot these facts.[7]

The convention was that all officers were gentlemen. Therefore they were equal in honour. Since this was not in fact the case, angry words often led to slurs upon honour. In the army a colonel could look the other way while two officers quickly settled an 'affair of honour'. Aboard ship the idea of two officers muttering and polishing their pistols did not bear thinking about. Instead, the many rancours of the wardroom ended in trials in the captain's cabin.

Any warrant or commissioned officer could call for a court martial on any other officer. They did so in droves: gunners tried captains, midshipmen accused lieutenants, captains prosecuted surgeons. Often two officers lodged simultaneous accusations against each other. Each would list the other's breaches of duty and complain about the names he was called. The court went into these cases in great detail.

There was an automatic court martial of the captain and officers whenever a ship was captured, lost at sea or badly damaged. This could happen to anyone. A captain could be judge one month and defendant the next. Men were broken in rank or 'discharged the service' for serious mistakes. However, it was important to the judges that no officer be punished unfairly, and such cases were considered in great technical detail. By and large officers had fair trials.

It was different for seamen. The officer faced a jury of his peers; the seaman faced a jury of his prosecutor's peers.[8] Even so, justice was not entirely blind. The methods of the court were rough and ready rather than legalistic.[9] But there was a certain blunt concern with the truth.

Marine John Longmead, for example, testified at the trial of the mutineers on the *Excellent*. He told the court what he had seen when he went below decks with the captain to suppress the mutiny. The court asked, 'Did it strike you that the Prisoner Evans' conduct was such that if you had been given the order to fire you would have picked him off first man?' To which Longmead answered, 'In [unreadable] I would have shot him.'[10]

That answer earned Evans a sentence of 800 lashes. Luckily, he was later pardoned. It was not the sort of evidence a clever lawyer would have allowed on shore. But it went to the heart of the matter.

Hearsay evidence was used all the time, and sometimes the judges were clearly prejudiced. The Excellents were tried by a court chaired by their commodore. Despite all this, there was always a chance of acquittal.

Sometimes seamen were charged with violating a specific article of war. Mostly men were just tried for what they had done. It was assumed that all reasonable officers would see where the crime lay. Thus in 1803 Marine John Johnson was tried for 'threatening the life of the person who stopped his grog'. George Watts of the *Trident* was charged with 'endeavouring to traduce the character of his captain by sticking up a paper in the waist [of the ship] and exciting the ship's company'. In 1808 James Seymour stood accused of 'making use of horrid expressions'.[11]

The judges tried to be fair. Both officers and men usually thought theft and murder were wrong. 'Buggery', however, was another matter: the men don't seem to have considered it a crime and hardly ever reported it; the officers were ambivalent. The penalty was death so the officers were usually very careful to establish the truth before convicting.

Desertion trials were common. The men were all for desertion. The officers for their part had to punish it severely or they would have no Navy. Here at least the offence was plain. Men were seldom framed for desertion and when the charge came to trial the court could observe the forms of law scrupulously.

When an officer confronted an angry sailor or a muttering demonstration he usually reacted with a tantrum or a flogging. On the other hand, if he was very angry or very frightened he would send the offenders for trial. A captain did not do this lightly. All the captains in port had to attend a court martial. The only escape was to send the ship's surgeon to testify that illness prevented attendance. A trial took up most of the day. If it was complicated or there were several defendants, it could go on for days, leaving ships immobilized. Some captains wanted to get back to their ships; many captains wanted to use their time in port in other, more recreational ways. The court martial records sometimes suggest that the captains are getting restive. In 1796 the prosecutor took 23 days to put his bumbling case against the mutineers of the *Defiance*. The court kept trying to hurry him.[12]

So officers did not always take kindly to attending a trial when the captain could have ordered 50 lashes and had done with it. Sometimes they discharged men, the case 'not proven'. Quite often they convicted but ordered only 50 lashes. This must have been a reproof to the captain.

If the captain usually avoided a court martial, a sailor was crazy to ask for one. On the *Macedonian* the

> drummer, being seized up for some petty offence, demanded, what no captain can refuse, to be tried by a court-martial, in the hope, probably, of escaping altogether. The officers laughed among each other, and when, a few days afterwards, the poor affrighted man offered to withdraw the demand and take six dozen lashes, they coolly remarked, 'The drummer is sick of his bargain.' He would have been a wiser man had he never made it; for the court-martial sentenced him to receive two hundred lashes through the fleet: – a punishment ostensibly for his first offense, but really for his insolence (?) in demanding a trial by court-martial.[13]

So most cases of 'insolence', 'contempt' and 'horrid language' were settled on shipboard, although some did end in a court martial. In these cases the majority of accused seamen were convicted. But some did get off. And the judges behaved with considerable respect for justice.

There was a catch. William Blake put it well: 'One law for the ox and the lion is oppression.' The court was careful to establish that the prisoner was guilty of the offence. But the offence *itself* was often resistance to authority. That is why a court martial could be both scrupulously fair and brutally repressive. The law was no ass, but it was a shark. This was very clear in the great show trials of mutineers like the Cullodens.

The ten defendants were tried one by one. Francis Watts was first. The evidence was damning: if anybody was a ringleader, it was Watts. A lawyer 'friend' helped Watts draw up a seven-page defence. Watts signed it with his mark. It was a clever legal effort – not the sort of thing to appeal to sea captains.

Watts and his friend called three witnesses. Captain Pakenham testified that Watts had come up willingly at the end.[14] Seaman John Edwards lied in his teeth for the sake of his berthmate. He said Watts had a black eye from having his hammock cut down at the start of the mutiny, Watts kept wanting to go on deck, and so on. The court questioned him. Edwards admitted that he had kissed the book, sworn the oath and carried arms. But he had been forced to do it. He hadn't seen anybody and knew no ringleaders or corporals. The court record continues:

> The court was cleared and agreed that the witnesses should be informed that there is a wide difference between the impious attempts to force upon him an illegal and unbinding Oath, and the solemn legal and awful Oath he had in the presence of God and Court lawfully and fully taken . . . and should he be hardy enough still to persist in his Prevarication, that the Course of Law in such Case should be pursued.

Note that the court assumes the Good Lord is present in

the captain's cabin but He cannot hear oaths sworn between decks. Note also a sneaking respect for Edwards's loyalty. The court speaks of him being *hardy* enough to persist. He was hardy: they threatened him with three months in the Marshalsea Prison; Edwards prevaricated a bit more. The court gave up and dismissed him.

The court was to have the same problem with several other witnesses. The seamen seemed to have difficulty in telling the difference between oaths to their shipmates and oaths to their officers. Then again, perhaps they did make a distinction. Nevertheless, the threat may have had an effect. Watts called only one more witness: Lieutenant Howard gave him a good character.

The second defendant was James Johnston. He had been the spokesman in negotiations and had written the letter. Like Watts, he was as good as dead. Two seamen lied loyally in his defence. The master-at-arms gave him a good character.

Cornelius Sullivan was the third defendant. He was not a ringleader. On the first night he was 'in liquor' and pitched in enthusiastically to drive the skulkers above decks. That night he was angry, loud and obscene; the following days he was sober and quiet.

Joseph Curtain was the fourth defendent. He too had been drunk and driven men on deck. He had taunted Whitter about the empty pistols. Seaman Dennis McCarty testified for the defence. He said Curtain had been asleep at the start of the mutiny and had been cut down in his hammock.

Seaman Maurice Dunn confirmed this. The court cross-questioned Dunn. They encouraged him to name names. He would not. The court was cleared. They brought Dunn back in again. The 'Act of Parliament respecting prevarication was read to him'. The court then questioned him closely:

Q. Was you watched?

A. Yes.

Q. How came you to the gun room?

A. When the rest was relieved . . .

Q. What were your orders as sentry?

A. Not to let any man up or down.

Q. Who gave you those orders?

A. The man that I relieved.

Q. Who did you relieve?

A. I cannot tell. I have no memory at all.

Q. Who relieved you?

A. I can't recollect, I can't call to mind the man . . .

Q. Who went the rounds with a lanthorn in his hand?

A. A great many.

Q. Can you recollect one?

A. No.

The fencing went on and on. Finally, the court stopped the trial for a few minutes to sentence Dunn to three months in the Marshalsea prison. This was the maximum sentence for lying in court.

It was an odd punishment. For other offences on shipboard a man was almost always flogged or hanged. Perhaps the officers were embarrassed or ashamed to flog a man for perjury in front of his shipmates, for they would admire his loyalty and there might be trouble.

After Dunn had been sentenced, Curtain said he had nothing more to offer in his defence. He threw himself on the mercy of the court. It was not forthcoming.

The next defendent was David Hyman. Seaman William Campbell was the first witness for the prosecution. He said Hyman was in charge of placing sentries on one watch. He also seriously implicated Watts and Johnston, whose cases had already been tried.

At this point the court was cleared yet again. The captains agreed to sentence all the prisoners seen so far: they sentenced Watts, Sullivan, Johnston and Curtain to death. They did not tell anybody of their verdict until the end of the trial. After that, they privately decided the fate of each defendant as his case finished.

They returned to Hyman. He was clearly a ringleader. His defence was that he had been asleep at the start of the mutiny. The master had beaten him awake.[15] One of his mates testified that Hyman had wanted to be on deck the whole time. Hyman did *not* call any officers to give him a good character. The court sentenced Hyman to death but recommended mercy. I will return later to the reasons for this verdict.

After Hyman came Jeremiah Collins. Several witnesses said he had been an implacable militant and had repeatedly threatened to blow up the ship. Collins offered no defence. Nor did he throw himself on the mercy of the court. Perhaps he felt it was useless. Perhaps he would not give them the satisfaction. The verdict was death.

Samuel Triggs, the 'corporal of the gun', was next. The evidence against him was damning. His defence was simple: 'That these things had been falsely sworn against him.' Seaman William Kelly spoke for the defence. Kelly said that on the last day of the mutiny Pakenham had spoken to the people. Then Triggs had said that they had better go on deck, that if their Musquets were fired they should all be hanged and the longer they stayed the worse it was for them. Nobody had opposed this, and the ship's company had gone on deck.

Triggs added the testimony of several officers to his character. Troubridge and the boatswain spoke well of him.

Lieutenant Nash of the *Royal Sovereign* had served in the *Cumberland* with him for three years and thought well of Triggs. Pakenham said that Triggs had been submissive when the men came up. The pistol-toting Lieutenant Whitter even said he had ben planning to recommend Triggs for promotion.[16] All these good characters may have weighed with the court. They sentenced Triggs to death but recommended mercy.

In his original letter to the admiral Troubridge had written that he was sending seven men for trial. Then he crossed out seven and wrote 'ten'.[17] It's probable that the three extra men were the last three to be tried. Certainly the case against them was thinner.

James Leader was the first of the three. The only evidence against him was that he had been a sentry on the last day. His defence was that he had been much disguised in liquor the first night of the mutiny. He knew nothing until he woke up the next morning. He then discovered that his hammock had been cut down during the night. He had been asleep on the deck. From then on he was trapped below. He was acquitted.

John Morrish was the next defendant. He entered the ship as an ordinary seaman. Four months later he was demoted to landsman. Later he was promoted able seaman. He was 24 and came from Whitstone in Devon. He was probably bred to the sea but offended the officers somehow after joining.

Several witnesses said he had been a sentry below. So had 252 other mutineers. The testimony of Midshipman Henry Richardson was more dangerous. Richardson said that at two on Friday morning Morrish had presented a musket up the hatchway in a menacing manner. He had then called the midshipman a 'lopsided dog driving bugger'. The court questioned Richardson closely. They had trouble believing he could have recognized Morrish in the faint light from a distant lantern.

Morrish denied everything. He claimed he was forced to remain below. He called several officers to speak to his character. Lieutenant Whitter said he knew nothing against Morrish, a standard phrase usually taken to mean that the officer could not care less if the prisoner swung. But Lieutenant Owen said the prisoner had behaved well before the mutiny, while Lieutenant Harward gave him a good character and said he had served for two years in the launch. (This was a position of trust because it was easy to desert from the launch.) The master's mate said he 'has always behaved well – an orderly sober man, very much so'. The boatswain gave him a good character. The master-at-arms said, 'I know the man to be a quiet civil man since I have been in the ship, and never disorderly in any shape when I have known him'.

Confronted with such saintliness, the court recalled Midshipman Richardson. They questioned him closely and established that there had been a large crowd around the hatch:

Q. Are you confident that it was sufficiently light for the Prisoner to discern your person at the time you say he presented the Musquet at you and used the language that you have delivered to the court upon oath?

A. It was, and he made use of the expression 'I see you' . . . He said it was the midshipman who came lately to the ship – the captain's son-in-law.

The court sentenced Morrish to death with a recommendation of mercy. The judges could be pretty sure the result would be a pardon. His good character may have impressed them. Probably they did not believe Midshipman Richardson but did not wish to give him the lie direct.

The last defendant was James Bartlett, a 25-year-old able seaman from Totnes in Devon. The main witness against Bartlett was a boy named David Wallace. Wallace said Bartlett had stood sentry duty. He said no more against anybody. The court asked:

Q. Did the prisoner swear you?
A. I cannot tell who swore me.

The court did not press him. The boy had stated the matter clearly: 'I cannot'. They no longer had the heart to bully stubborn witnesses.

Bartlett put up a long and spirited defence with the help of the same lawyer who had helped Watts. Bartlett said he had been in the Navy for five years and had been expecting promotion to boatswain. Why should he wreck his career? He had been forced to join the mutineers.

Captain Troubridge and Lieutenant Whitter confirmed that they had been thinking of promoting him while other officers gave him a good character. The court acquitted Bartlett.

Then all the defendants were called into court. The sentences were read out to them. Five were sentenced to death. Three were sentenced to death but recommended to mercy. Two were discharged. Sometimes it's easy to see the logic of the judges. Bartlett got very good characters and Leader was accused of very little. Morrish received excellent characters and may have been falsely accused. But Hyman and Triggs were clearly in it up to their necks. They didn't receive particularly good characters. Why did they receive mercy?

We must understand that all big mutiny trials followed the same pattern: some prisoners were hanged; some received lesser sentences; some got off. Everybody knew this would be the pattern before the trial began. The executions displayed the full fury of the law; the acquittals demonstrated the fairness of the law; the lesser punishments showed the compassion of the authorities.[18]

The executions were intended as a theatre of terror. They were not without effect. Listen to Leech:

'Why did not your crew rise in resistance to such cruelty?' is a question which has often been proposed to me, when relating these facts to my American friends. To talk of mutiny on shore is an easy matter; but to excite it on shipboard is to rush on to certain death. Let it be known that a man has dared to breathe the idea, and he is sure to swing at the yard-arm. Some of our men once saw six mutineers hanging at the yard-arm at once, in a ship whose crew exhibited the incipient beginnings of mutiny. Let mutiny be successful, the government will employ its whole force, if needful, in hunting down the mutineers; their blood, to the last drop, is the terrible retribution it demands for the offence. That demand is sure to be met, as was the case with the crew of the Hermione frigate, and the crew of the ill-fated Bounty, whose history is imprinted on the memory of the whole civilized world. With such tragedies flitting before our eyes, who need ask why we did not resist?[19]

Leech is mistaken here. Only four of the *Bounty* mutineers were hanged. Nine escaped to Pitcairn and two were pardoned after the trial. The men who chose to sail away with Fletcher Christian had a better survival rate than the men who got into the launch with Captain Bligh. Again, 24 of the Hermiones were hanged; almost 130 of them got away. Mutiny did not mean certain death.[20]

This made it all the more important for the Royal Navy to dramatize its revenge. The sailors might remember victory on the *Windsor Castle* and at Spithead. They might forget the men who got away. They would surely remember the agitator on the *Marlborough* turning a slow purple as his shipmates hauled on the ropes.[21] They would not forget the skeletons hanging in chains at the entrance to Port Royal harbour. The officers hoped their hate would seem all-powerful. For many, Leech included, it did.

Nevertheless, justice was often tempered with mercy. Nicol, for instance, remembered a shipmate on the *Surprise*. We pick up his story just after the British have captured the American ship *Jason*:

A marine of the name of Kennedy, . . . an intelligent lad, and well-behaved, was a great favourite with the surgeon. They used to be constantly together reading and acquiring information; they came from the same place, had been at school together, and were dear friends; Kennedy's relations were in a respectable line of life. I never learned the cause of his filling his present lowly station. As it fell out, poor Kennedy was placed sentinel over the spirit-room of the Jason. He was, as I have said, an easy kind of lad, and had not been long from home. He allowed the men to carry away the spirits; and they were getting fast drunk, when the prize-master perceived it. Kennedy was relieved, and sent on board the Surprise, and next morning put in irons on board the Europa, the admiral's ship, where he was tried by a court-martial, and sentenced to be hanged on the fore-yard-arm. His offense, no doubt, was great, for the men would all have been so much the worse of liquor in a short time, that the Americans could have recovered the Jason with ease. Yet we were all sorry for him, and would have done anything in our power to redeem him from his present melancholy situation. His friend the surgeon was inconsolable, and did everything in his power. He drew up a petition to the admiral for pardon, stating his former good behaviour, his youth, and good connections, and everything he could think of in his favour; but all would not do. He was taken to the place of execution, the rope round his neck, the match was lit, the clergyman at his post; we were all aloft and upon deck to see him run up to the yard-arm, amidst the smoke of the gun, the signal of death. When every one looked for the command to fire, the admiral was pleased to pardon him. He was sent on board the Surprise, more like a corpse than a living man; he could scarce walk, and seemed indifferent to everything on board, as if he knew not whether he was dead or alive. He continued thus for a long time, scarce speaking to any one; he was free, and did no duty, and was the same on board as a passenger.[22]

The surgeon's petition was crucial. Eighteenth-century courts on land and at sea paid careful attention to petitions from men and women of their own class. Kennedy's good connections counted for a lot, too. Middle-class boys seldom went to the scaffold. In every court it was always important who would speak for the defendant.[23]

This was the reason for prisoners calling officers to give them a 'character'. The court often gave a man's good character as the reason for recommending mercy. At courts martial men never received bad characters. Presumably a man's enemies refused to testify or were not asked. No sort of character could have saved Watts or Johnston of the *Culloden*. But it helped some of the others. It certainly saved Bartlett.

At the start of a trial the officers could bring cases and testify away the lives of their men. At the end of the trial they could demonstrate their paternal concern. The fierce captain could be balanced by the kind surgeon. The surviving defendants returned to the ship's company owing their lives to individual officers. In the same way, before a flogging an officer often intervened to plead for a man. Both customs worked to bind men to their officers.

Everybody in a mutiny trial knew that some defendants would perish and some survive. Cases were often heard separately. Each man faced the prosecutor on his own, so each usually mounted an individual defence. You might expect these circumstances to eat away at the solidarity of the defendants. On the *Excellent*, for instance, Matt Loyal said that John Lovell Crabbe led him on.[24] This sort of thing was blessedly rare, however. Any mutineer could usually avoid a trial by turning king's evidence. The defendants were the men who had refused to betray their mates.

The court hoped its procedures would reinforce faith in the law. Even here, in the irritated bowels of naval discipline, we can see captains straining for the truth.

The men, on the other hand, felt less respect for the majesty of the law. The solidarity of the lower-deck witnesses was remarkable. It was not exceptional. It occurs over and over again in other trials. Troubridge had to use the same few witnesses again and again. One of them was his personal steward, John Carnes. Solomon Bostock was another. He had opposed the mutiny from the start and was trapped below. After the trial he was promoted to boatswain and transferred to another ship. Two marines were regular witnesses. They had been among the six marines stuck below during the mutiny and, after it was over, must have felt vulnerable and isolated. Nonetheless, their testimony often pointed to innocence rather than guilt. Furthermore many sailors bore false witness for the defence.

This was normal. They didn't take a sacred oath lightly. Mutineers, trade unionists and revolutionaries all used solemn oaths for safety's sake. The lower-deck oath on the *Culloden* was intended as a mystical counterweight to any courtroom oath. Clearly, even the judges on the court understood this. They treated the men's oath with an ambivalent and exasperated but implicit respect. Even without their oath, the men would have relied on their solidarity: some things mattered more to a British seaman than God and Hell.

The Cullodens remained below for three days *after* the Admiralty had agreed to refit the ship. They would not come up without a promise that no man would face a court martial. Later they may have made pious statements to the court about justice and mercy. The captains may have done their limited best to deliver honest and compassionate verdicts. But the refusal of 300 to surrender their ringleaders speaks volumes. They had rumbled the 'rule of law'.

We can understand the sentences on the Cullodens if we bear in mind the purpose and form of the trial. Troubridge presented the defendants in a rough order of guilt. This was common practice and would be readily understood by the court. Watts the ringleader came first. Johnston the spokesman was second. After them came two angry drunks: Sullivan and Curtain. Then in the middle of Hyman's trial the court decided to sentence the previous defendants. All four got death.

With four men's blood on their hands, the court recommended Hyman to mercy. Collins was the next defendant. He stubbornly refused to ask for mercy. He was 40, much older than the others. Collins must have known that some would survive and some would be hanged. Maybe he hoped that by himself reaching for the noose, he could save another. The court had no choice in his case but death.

By now they had sentenced five of the ten defendants to death. It was time for moderation. Two of the next four were acquitted; two were recommended to mercy. Even Samuel Triggs, the 'corporal of the gun', survived.

The court-martial delivered its verdict on 20 December. Three days later the Admiralty transferred the 30 potential troublemakers to other ships. Christmas seems to have passed quietly. In the next two weeks five men were flogged. On 9 January the ship's company received six months pay for each man. They could get drunk and, perhaps, happy.[25]

Four days later the eight 'guilty' mutineers were brought on board in irons. The Cullodens assembled to witness punishment. Samuel Triggs, John Morrish and David Hyman were pardoned. They returned to the ship's company. Francis Watts, James Johnston, Cornelius Sullivan, Joseph Curtain and Jeremiah Collins were hanged.[26]

There is some evidence that the *Culloden* was not a happy ship afterwards. In the first nine months of 1793 Captain Rich had flogged 21 Cullodens; two of them had received 24 lashes. In the seven months after the mutiny Troubridge flogged 39 men; 15 of them received 24 lashes.[27]

Perhaps these figures show the Cullodens were right to worry about Lieutenant Whitter. Perhaps Troubridge was trying to cow them. Or perhaps he was reacting to a higher level of unrest. Twelve days after the hangings William Lamle got two dozen lashes for leaving the launch when on duty, maybe an attempt at desertion. William Fourneaux got a dozen for the same offence. Joseph Cane also got a dozen lashes for drunkenness and fighting. Three days later John Gardner received two dozen lashes for 'throwing a shot at the time of the punishment on the 25 inst.' This is a very light sentence for an offence which would usually merit a court martial. Troubridge was in no position to expose unrest in his crew by ordering courts martial.

Many men simply 'ran'. In the nine months immediately after the mutiny, there were 19 successful desertions and ten men were flogged for leaving the ship's boats.[28] John Carnes tried twice to desert. He was Troubridge's personal steward and had testified extensively for the prosecution. He may have found life on board unhappy. The first time he was caught an understanding Troubridge let him off with six lashes; the second time it was two dozen. Maurice Dunn returned at the end of March from three months in the Marshalsea prison for prevarication in defence of Francis Watts. On Mayday 1795 Dunn ran and got clean away.

The *Culloden* never did convoy duty again. Nor was it sent to the West Indies. For several months the Cullodens were in and out of harbours on the English coast, keeping the shipwrights and caulkers busy. By summer the Admiralty seems to have felt the *Culloden* was safe enough to be sent to join the Mediterranean fleet. The old ship was never again risked in mid Atlantic, however.[29]

The Cullodens spent five years in the Mediterranean. In July 1795 they saw action against the French fleet. They lost three men: two sailors and Lieutenant Whitter of the empty pistols. In February 1797 Troubridge led the British line into battle against the Spanish fleet at Cape St Vincent: 'Look at Troubridge,' shouted Admiral Jervis from his flagship, 'he tacks his ship to battle as if the eyes of all England were upon him; and would to God they were'. What made the feat all the more remarkable was that two days before Troubridge had accidentally collided with HMS *Colossus* 'sustaining damage which would have driven any other captain but Troubridge into harbour.'[30]

The Cullodens played no part in the mutinies of 1797. Admiral Jervis moved swiftly to forestall any possibility of rebellion, hanging four trouble-makers and two homosexuals as an example to the fleet. Three of them were executed on a Sunday. Vice-Admiral Thompson was sacked for protesting at the sacrilege. Nelson wrote, 'Had it been Christmas Day, instead of Sunday, I would have executed them.'[31]

In July 1797 one of Jervis's admirals inspected the *Culloden*. He said the ship was generally in a good state and fit for any service. There was a three-watch system: more restful for the men than a two-watch system. The men were in very good health. There was no favouritism in regard to pieces of meat from the ship's stores. Unfortunately, there was no bedding or sheets for the sick. But, he commented favourably, 'water gruel every morning for Breakfast, Articles of War read once a month'.[32] What more could a man ask?

Troubridge and Nelson became close friends. At the Battle of the Nile in 1798 the *Culloden* was twelfth in the line of 14 British ships. Fortunately, the first 11 ships into Aboukir Bay did not run aground on the shoal discovered by

Troubridge. Luckier still, his prompt signals warned off the two ships following. By the time the *Culloden* was afloat again the battle was over. Troubridge's chance for glory was gone.

In December 1799 the *Culloden* was sent to the relief of Malta, but ran aground on entering the harbour. Troubridge wrote to Nelson, 'I run on a rock in the middle of the Channel, the vagabonds who made it ought to be hung'.[33]

The *Culloden* could take no more. In August 1800 the old ship went into harbour for the last time.[34] Troubridge himself went on to greater things. He was smart, he was an excellent organizer, and his fiery attitude appealed to other officers. He had long been a favourite of Admiral Jervis. In 1801 Jervis, now Lord St. Vincent, became First Lord of the Admiralty. He took Troubridge with him to Whitehall as one of the Sea Lords. Troubridge had reached the pinnacle of his profession.

It couldn't last for ever, though. St Vincent was not just honest. That was bad enough. He was also offensive and aggressive in his attacks on naval corruption. When the Addington ministry fell in 1804, St Vincent and Troubridge went too. Troubridge, by now an admiral, was posted to the East Indies. There he served in unhappy rivalry with Admiral Pellew. The two admirals finally prevailed on Whitehall to split the command: Pellew was to have India and Troubridge the Cape.

Troubridge sailed from Madras for the Cape on 12 January 1807. Many felt that his flagship, the *Blenheim*, was not up to the voyage. The ship's captain begged Troubridge in vain not to take the risk. Perhaps Troubridge wanted to get away from Admiral Pellew quickly.

On 1 February the *Blenheim* ran into a cyclone off the coast of Madagascar. The brigs *Java* and *Harrier* accompanied the flagship. When the cyclone was over the *Harrier* was alone. Troubridge's son, himself captain of the *Greyhound*, was sent to search for his father. He found nothing. The French sent word they had found a few pieces of driftwood from the *Blenheim*.[35]

Hundreds of men and women had died because they put their trust in Troubridge's impetuous seamanship. The Cullodens had made their own decision about putting to sea. They lost only five men.

'The Point of Honour' by Cruikshank. A seaman is about to be flogged. The marines are drawn up on the quarterdeck, the crew in the waist. The small boys in uniform are midshipmen.

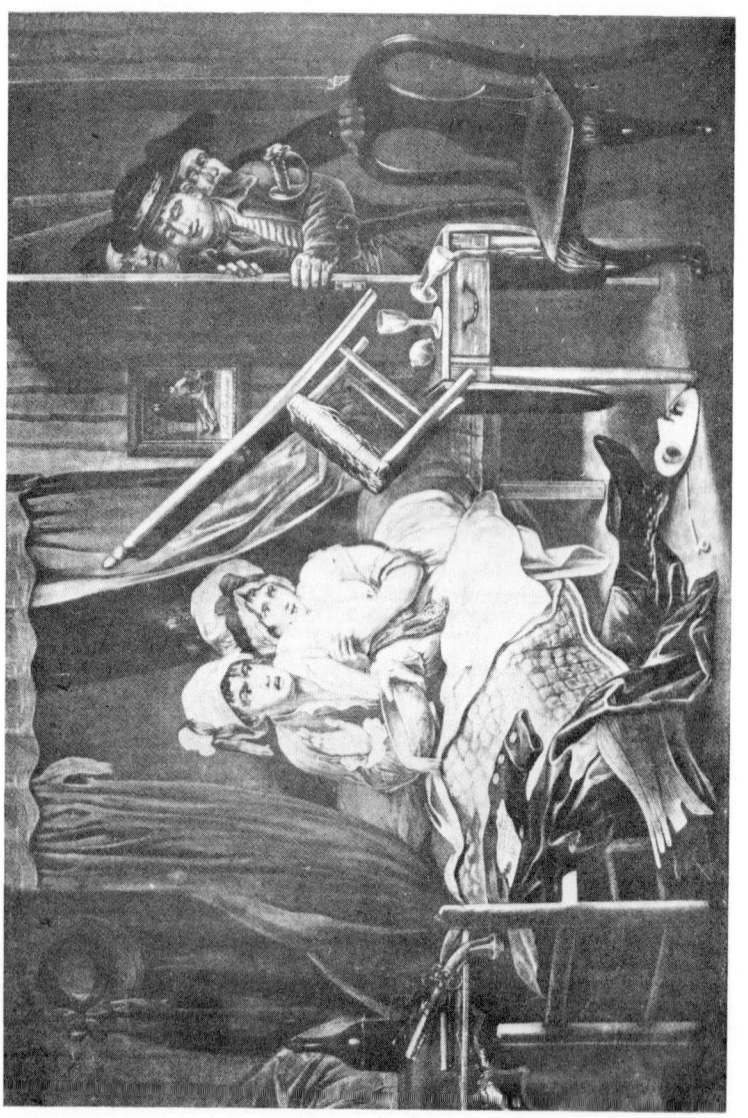

'An unwelcome visit from the press gang'

'Jack Spratt, the London 'Prentice, carried off by the Pressgang'

The enraged Captain Thomas Troubridge of *HMS Colloden* kicks a French count.

Shore liberty. 'Sailors on a Cruise' by Cruikshank.

Pub life. 'Sailors Carousing' by Cruikshank.

'Sailors Carousing' by Ibbetson. A sailor with his pay in his pocket immediately bought a watch and got drunk. The men in the front of the picture are about to fry their watches, a form of conspicuous consumption.

John Nicol, aged 67. He was the author of *The Life and Adventures of John Nicol, Mariner.*

Mary Anne Talbot, in the dress of a male sailor. She was the author of *The Surprising Adventures of Mary Anne Talbot, Related by Herself.*

A grimmer vision of the press gang by Morland.

# 7

## 'My constant prayer to heaven is that my daughters may never step a foot on board of a man-of-war'

The Cullodens mutinied in 1794. In 1795 there was another rising on the *Defiance*. Understanding what happened on the *Defiance* requires some background on forecastle life. It is time to turn to grog, women and song.

The Royal Navy expected its sailors to drink. The Navy provided the drink free. Ships' crews close to home drank beer; in the Mediterranean they drank wine; everywhere else they drank rum. One man's daily ration was a gallon of beer or a pint of wine or a half-pint of rum. Half the ration was served at noon and half at four in the afternoon. So each man had four pints of beer for lunch and four pints at tea-time, or four double rums at lunch and four double rums for tea. Of course, the beer and rum were somewhat stronger then than now. In terms of what you get in a modern pub, they were drinking five pints or five double rums twice a day.[1]

Boys got a half-ration free until they were 18. If they had any money they could buy the other half. Officers were entitled to the usual ration *and* their own wine in the wardroom. The rum was mixed with water, normally in the proportions of three parts of water to one part of rum. This did not mean that the rum was diluted: the water was added *after* the full ration had been measured out.

The Navy had taken its rum neat until the 1740s, when Admiral Vernon introduced the practice of mixing in water. He hoped that the sailors would drink more slowly and get less drunk. Vernon always wore an overcoat made out of a cloth called 'grogam', and his men called him 'Old Grog'. His new drink was also called 'grog'.

Captain Home of the *Defiance* went further than Admiral Grogam and ordered his men to mix five parts of water to one part of rum. Sailors, however, had a strong sense of their traditional rights.[2] Their rations were provided and set by custom and the rules of the Navy. They felt entitled to refuse any changes in their allowance. They were especially attached to their grog, and they didn't like it tasting like weak piss.

Two hundred years ago people drank far more than they do now. But even then the Navy had a reputation. The popular image of Jack Tar ashore was an amiable drunk singing off-key with one arm round a prostitute and his brains pickled. While customs have changed since the eighteenth century, the human body has not: a man who drank the Navy's ration every day was an alcoholic.

A man-of-war was a community of 600 chronic alcoholics. Historians sometimes write as if this was glamorous. After 1815 the cold-water-and-icy-Christianity brigade gained a foothold below decks. Although they are hard people to sympathize with, there was a reason for their growing strength: alcohol in large quantities is simply not good for you. And as Hodgskin put it, 'There is no place in the world where personal safety is so much endangered as at sea.'[3]

The captain could order men to the guns right after grog had been served out. Drunken officers would angrily patrol a line of drunken men at the guns. Or the sails might have to be furled. Drunken men would race up swaying rigging and out on to yards that yawed in the wind. Mistakes and floggings were the common consequence. Remember how three men fell to their deaths on the *Hermione*? That happened at 6 p.m. Captain Pigot and all the officers and men were drunk.[4]

The officers all tolerated heavy drinking. Indeed most of them joined in. The reasons why the Navy provided booze are not far to seek. Sailors were largely pressed men. They were seldom allowed ashore. At sea a ship 100 feet long contained 500 bitter and sexually frustrated young men for months on end. They worked long hours at hard, cold, wet and degrading work. So they drank. And the officers realized, implicitly or explicitly, that it was easier to control them that way.

Bored sailors spent a lot of time thinking about drink. There were a hundred stratagems to get more and a thousand yarns about the stratagems. The most common trick was perfectly legal.

Each mess was a group of nine or so men who ate together at their own table below decks. Men chose their own mess. Some unpleasant people had to eat by themselves. Each man took it in turn to be cook for his mess. Among other things the cook drew the rum ration for the whole mess. When he shared it out he kept for himself a special large measure: the 'plush'. On some ships this was almost half the ration. He could spend the day getting very drunk indeed.

Men also gave their ration to each other in exchange for a similar favour another day. There were innumerable ways of smuggling drink aboard. All these let the sailor achieve what he wanted most: oblivion. As Leech said, 'to be drunk is considered by almost every sailor to be the *acme* of sensual bliss'.[5]

Sailors drank more in port. The ship was full of women and they were expected to smuggle drink on board.

Sailors had no prejudice against women on board. In fact, on most ships the gunner was encouraged to bring his wife to sea. He berthed with the ships boys and it was hoped his wife could provide the boys with something of a mother's tender affections. It was also hoped she would shield them from the tender affections of the men.

Many petty officers and some favoured seamen were allowed to bring their wives. This was an indulgence permitted to good boys and could be withdrawn any time. In some cases these women were legal wives. In other cases they were port prostitutes who hitched up with a man for the voyage. John Nicol, for instance, was on the *Goliath* at the Battle of the Nile in 1798. He remembered the 'boys and women who carried the powder' for the guns. There was a woman from Leith who died of her wounds and another woman from Edinburgh who 'bore a son in the heat of the action'.[6]

Of course many sailors preferred men to women. Then as now, many must have been drawn to the sea because it provided a more supportive environment for homosexuals.[7] Many sailors must also have made do with what came to hand. It is impossible to tell how common this was. There is one suggestive habit of speech: *the* insult between sailors was 'you bugger'. Again and again the phrase crops up in the mouths of officers yelling at the men, sailors joshing each other or starting a fight, men searching for a word to emphasize an oath. Many sailors may have disapproved of sex with men, but the possibility was clearly much on their minds.

Still, for the majority of men ports meant women. The press had torn them from their families. Sailors were often pressed off merchantmen as they returned from several years' voyage to the east. Unless he deserted a man usually served from the date of impressment until the declaration of peace. A man impressed in 1793 remained on board until the peace of 1802. A man impressed in 1803 would serve ten years. Some men were unlucky. They were not discharged during the peace of 1802 and served right through the wars. Because they were not usually allowed ashore in home waters, their families had to come to them.

This they did. In port the ship was full of aged fathers, weeping mothers, comradely brothers and sisters. A pressed man's children would come aboard to see him. When Valentine Joyce of Belfast served in the Channel Fleet his wife lived in Portsmouth. This must have been common, for the Channel Fleet spent much of the winter in port. A man and his wife could make love on board ship. But they usually had to do it in a room with three hundred other people. So they might sneak off for a little privacy underneath the guns – a practice that's given us the phrase 'son of a gun'.

On pay-day, which might be only once every three or four years, most sailors would not have their wives with them. The Admiralty only paid men in home ports. At times it did not pay them for three or four years. Jack Nastyface describes a typical occasion:

> After having moored our ship, swarms of boats came round us; . . . a great many of them were freighted with cargoes of ladies, a sight that was truly gratifying and a great treat; for our crew, consisting of six hundred and upwards, nearly all young men, had seen but one woman on board for eighteen months, and that was the daughter of one of the Spanish chiefs . . .

So soon as these boats were allowed to come alongside, the seamen flocked down pretty quick, one after the other, and brought their choice up, so that in the course of the afternoon, we had about four hundred and fifty on board.

Of all the human race, these poor young creatures are the most pitiable; the ill-usage and degradation they are driven to submit to are indescribable; but from habit they become callous, indifferent as to delicacy of speech and behaviour, and so totally lost to all sense of shame, that they seem to retain no quality which properly belongs to woman, but the shape and name. When we reflect that these unfortunately deluded victims to our passions, might at one time have been destined to be the valuable companions and comforts of man, but now so fallen: in these cooler moments of meditation, what a charge is raised against ourselves; we cannot reproach them for their abject condition, lest this startling question should be asked of us, who made us so?

On the arrival of any man of war in port, these girls flock down to the shore, where boats are always ready; and here may be witnessed a scene, somewhat similar to the trafficking for slaves in the West Indies. As they approached a boat . . . [the boatman] before they step on board surveys them from stem to stern . . . [He] carefully culls out the best looking, and the most dashingly dressed; and, in making up his complement for a load, it often happens that he refuses to take some of them, observing (very politiely) and usually with some vulgar oath; to one, that she is *too old*: to another, that she is *too ugly*; and that he shall not be able *to sell them*; and he'll be d——d if he has any notion of having his trouble for nothing. The only apology that can be made for the savage conduct of these unfeeling brutes is, that they run a chance of not being permitted to carry a cargo alongside, unless it make a good shew-off; for it has been known, that, on approaching a ship, the officer in command has so far forgot himself as to order the waterman to push off – that he should not bring such a cargo of d——d ugly devils on board, and that he should not allow any of his men to have them. At this ungentlemanly rebuff, the waterman lays up on his oars a-while, hangs his lip, musing on his mishap; and in his heart, no doubt cursing and doubly cursing the quarterdeck fool, and gradually pulls round to shore again. And the girls not sparing of their epithets on the occasion. Here the waterman is a loser, for he takes them conditionally: that is, if they are made choice of, or what he calls *sold*, he receives three shillings each; and if not, then no pay.

Thus these poor unfortunates are taken to market like cattle; and whilst this system is observed, it cannot with truth be said, that the slave-trade is abolished in England.

I am now happily laid up in matrimonial harbour, blest in a wife and several children, and my constant prayer to heaven is, that my daughters may never step a foot on board of a man-of-war.[8]

A ship in harbour carried a lot of women. When the *Royal George* went down at Spithead in 1782, 300 women drowned. Or take Richardson's ship when it received a visit from Princess Caroline in 1806. The whole ship was carefully cleaned beforehand and 'hundreds' of women were ordered to hide below until the royal guest had gone:

> As her Royal Highness was going round the decks and viewing the interior, she cast her eyes down the main hatchway, and there saw a number of girls peeping up at her. 'Sir Richard,' she said, 'you told me there were no women on board the ship, but I am convinced there are, as I have seen them peeping up from that place, and am inclined to think they are put down there on my account.' She told the captain to let the women up. They lined the booms and gangways to view the princess.[9]

Many sailors married prostitutes. Sometimes it was only for a voyage. Often it was in the hope of a life-long love. This may seem strange. Captain Glascock tells what he takes to be a funny story about a sailor in love:

> A seaman, whose ship was on the point of sailing from Spithead, was extremely solicitous to obtain permission to go on shore, for the purpose of leading to the altar one of the chaste sirens of *Sallyport*. [Glascock means a prostitute.]
> Joe, during the time the ship's company were at dinner, was seen dodging about the decks, 'backing and filling', for a favourable opportunity to make his simple appeal to the sterner feelings of the first lieutenant. He at length, however, appeared to have 'screwed-up his courage to the sticking place,' and made an effort to go aft . . . In his approach to the lieutenant, he bore more the appearance of a criminal leading out to execution, than of an anxious bridegroom on the eve of the consummation

of all his eager wishes. But he felt it was too late to retract, so he proceeded to open the business, with an awkward inflexion of the body, and a twist of his shoulders, as a token of profound respect. As yet a word had not escaped him, and it appeared still problematical whether, without encouragement, his timidity would not compel him to carry his secret with him to the grave.

His head hung down, and, except that now and then he stole an anxious and furtive glance at the lieutenant, to help him out at guessing how the 'wind lay', his wide eyes were intently fixed on the buckle of his hat-band, which he alternately twiddled with the fore finger and thumb of both hands, whilst in a suppliant tone, he hesitatingly began, 'Please, sir, I've a bit of a favour to ax.' – 'Well, my man, what is it?' replied the lieutenant. – 'I know', rejoined Joe, 'It's more almost nor a man can expect' . . . alternately shifting his legs and jerking out his words.

[Finally Joe brings himself to say what he wants.]

'The girl be d——d!' exclaimed the lieutenant; 'you don't mean to say, you want to be spliced to that bare-faced hussy that was aboard?' – 'Yes, i' you please, sir; the strands are unlaid.' – 'Unlaid!' said the lieutenant; 'You deserve to have the cat laid on your back for being such an infernal fool. Can you offer,' continued he, in a somewhat more pacified tone, 'the least plausible reason for even thinking of marrying so common a strumpet?' – 'Yes, sir,' said Joe, replying more promptly than hitherto, and with an air of self-satisfaction, indicating hopes of carrying conviction as well as his point, 'yes, sir; 'Kase whenever the ship comes into port, and *she's aboard of another*, I can always shove alongside and *claim her as my own*!'[10]

Joe stands on the quarterdeck at a loss for words, his hat in his hand and his eyes fixed on the buckle of its band. Captain Glascock gaves an accurate picture of how men behaved on the quarterdeck. This is what the court martial judges meant when they asked if a man had petitioned in a respectful manner. A sailor faced a flogging or worse if he looked his officer in the eye and spoke like a man. 'Joe' is a slave. Glascock is making fun of him for behaving like a slave.

When Glascock told that story in the wardroom, they must have laughed so hard they fell on the floor. Officers could go ashore when they wanted and partake of whatever pleasure they chose. Joe was trapped on board with sirens of Sallyport. Lonely folk grab love where they can and return a fierce and awkward commitment.

And sailors and prostitutes had much in common. A man escaped unhappy love or unemployment by running away to sea. Sailors were often the bad boys whose wild spirits could not be contained in the village. A dishonoured woman often moved from unhappy love to prostitution. Women were forbidden male jobs and wild girls could not run away to sea. For them it was the suffocating prison of domestic service or the degradation of the bum-boats.

There were practical advantages to marrying a sailor. For instance, a wife could receive a portion of her husband's pay. In Portsmouth a working woman found it convenient to be able to present her marriage lines: the mayor had periodic rushes of blood to the head when he tried to clean up the town by banishing all single women.[11]

It's hard to find out exactly what went on below decks in ports. At the time writers used vague phrases like 'furies and harpies', 'degradation' and the like. But it's clear that discipline was relaxed. There was much less work to do. The men had the lower deck to themselves. The officers did not trespass there. The women smuggled drink on board, and the officers turned a blind eye. There was a party atmosphere.

Christmas in port was a particularly drunken feast. Leech eventually married a nice Yankee Methodist and turned temperance. He looked back with disapproval:

> The Sabbath was also a day of sensuality. True, we sometimes had the semblance of religious services, when the men were summoned aft to hear the captain read the morning service from the church prayer-book; but usually it was observed more as a day of revelry than of worship. But at Christmas our ship presented a scene such as I had never imagined. The men were permitted to have their 'full swing'. Drunkenness ruled the ship. Nearly every man, with most of the officers, were in a state of beastly intoxication at night. Here, some were fighting, but were so insensibly drunk, they hardly knew whether they struck the guns of their opponents; yonder, a party were singing libidinous or baccanalian songs, while all were laughing, cursing, swearing or hallooing; confusion reigned in glorious triumph. It was the very chaos of humanity.[12]

Christmas was special. But the officers generally encouraged a relaxation when a ship was in port. They turned a blind eye to drink-smuggling – an indulgence which could always be withdrawn. The men also valued singing. Leech remembered 'Happy Jack':

By such means as these, sailors contrive to keep up their spirits amidst constant causes of depression and misery. One is a good singer, another can spin tough forecastle yarns, while a third can crack a joke with sufficient point to call out roars of laughter. But for these interludes, life in a man-of-war, with severe officers, would be absolutely intolerable; mutiny or desertion would mark the voyages of every such ship. Hence, officers in general highly value your jolly, merry-making, don't care sort of seaman. They know the effect of their influence in keeping away discontented thoughts from the minds of a ship's company.

One of these official favourites paid our frigate a visit while we lay at Lisbon. We had just finished breakfast, when a number of our men were seen running in high glee towards the main hatchway . . . The cause of their joy soon appeared in the person of a short, round-faced merry-looking tar, who descended the hatchway, amid the cries of 'Hurrah! here's Happy Jack!' As soon as the jovial little man had set his foot on the berth deck, he began a specimen of his verbal powers. The voice of song was as triumphant on board the *Macedonian*, as it was in the days of yore in the halls of Ossian. Every voice was hushed, all work was brought to stand still, while the crew gathered around their favourite, in groups, to listen to his unequalled performance. Happy Jack succeeded, while his visit lasted, in communicating his own joyous feelings to our people, and they parted from him that night with deep regret.

A casual visitor in a man-of-war, beholding the

song, the dance, the revelry of the crew, might judge them to be happy. But I know that these things are often resorted to, because they feel miserable, just to drive away dull care. They do it on the same principle as the slave population in the South [of the United States], to drown in sensual gratification the voice of misery that groans in the inner man – that lives within, speaking of the indignity offered to its high nature by the chain that eats beyond the flesh – discoursing of the rights of man, of liberty on the free hills of a happier clime: while amidst the gayest negro dance, not a heart among the laughing gang but would beat with high emotions, and seize the boon with indescribable avidity, should it be offered its freedom on the spot.[13]

In the Caribbean slaves planned their great revolts at happy parties which brought together slaves from different plantations. Something of the same sort happened on the *Defiance*.

# 8

## 'Liberty and no more five-water grog!'

On 29 September 1795 the 74-gun man-of-war, *Defiance*, sailed up the Firth of Forth and anchored in the Leith Roads near Edinburgh. The ship had been in the North Sea and off the coast of Norway for three months. The weather had been filthy.[1] The people of the *Defiance* were looking forward to shore leave.

It was Sunday morning as the ship sailed up the Forth. Landsman John Graham was writing up a journal for Midshipman Mudie. Like all midshipmen, Mudie was obliged to keep a copy of the ship's log. When he presented himself for his examination to pass as lieutenant, he would have to produce these logs. But Mudie had got behind by 20 days and was too lazy to do it himself. He asked assistant clerk Thomas Innes to copy it for him. Innes agreed. Then he 'jammed' his fingers, so he got John Graham to do some of his writing. Among the things Graham copied was Mudie's journal. He may have been paid for it, or he may have found it almost impossible to refuse. In any case, copying that journal later almost cost him his life.

Graham was 21 years old and came from Eastwhitton. Like many of the crew, he was a 'quota man'.[2] Captain Home had been raising men since early spring, but in July the admiral thought the ship still 'very indifferently manned.' He attributed this to the large number of men discharged to hospital, sick below, or run. Captain Home felt that the admiral blamed him.[3]

Home was not the only officer desperate for men in 1795. At the beginning of the war two years earlier the press gangs had swept the port. Now many experienced sailors were already in the Navy. Many of the ports seemed deserted and forlorn, with no young men on the streets. But the Navy was still expanding, as were the army and the militia. The Navy needed men, and it was draining a shrinking pool of skilled labour. The press gang alone would not provide the answer.

So in 1795 the government set up the 'quota' system. Each city or county had to raise so many men for the Navy each year. The local authorities paid a cash bounty to each man who signed up. This bounty varied from place to place and time to time. It was often quite large – five pounds, ten pounds or more. It appealed to men facing debtor's prison who could pay their creditors and go off to earn a sort of living. In the bad year of 1795 it appealed to men with hungry families. It may have tempted sailors who wanted a colossal blow-out before they shipped again. The magistrates sometimes supplemented the quota by giving poachers and revolutionaries a choice between transportation and the Navy.[4]

Captains did not like quota men. Naval historians have followed their lead. The traditional quota man is a puny, lousy, under-nourished, dirty thief: the scum of the streets and the sweepings of the prisons. He was more than likely infected with typhus or revolutionary ideas. He is sometimes held responsible for all the mutinies in the fleet.

The picture is unfair: the sailors already had some pretty naughty ideas. Furthermore, many quota men were able seamen bred to the sea. We should not think less of a man for getting into debt or stealing a chicken. But perhaps the captains found it difficult to rid themselves of a certain contempt for men who had *volunteered* for the Navy.

John Graham had signed up as part of the Whitby quota. Like the other quota men on the *Defiance*, he had collected the local bounty. But he also expected to collect the normal naval bounty paid to men when they volunteered. This had been denied to the Defiances. They were angry about it. The captain petitioned the admiralty on their behalf, but without success.[5]

The whole North Sea fleet had trouble raising men. The other ships had no complement of marines at all. But they did carry soldiers to do the job. The admiral complained that the soldiers were nearly useless, being either sick or incompetent.[6] The *Defiance* did not even have soldiers: this was crucial in the mutiny.

Every captain relied on the marines to control the ship. The Navy had sent Lieutenant Bligh to Tahiti without marines to make space for the breadfruit trees the *Bounty* was supposed to collect. When Bligh tried to get tough with his men, there were no marines to back him up. So his ferocious rage began to look like bluster, and the habit of power slipped through his fingers.[7]

Without marines and soldiers, there would be no sentries. So Captain Home had some of the people issued with small arms. From among them the master-at-arms selected various men to be 'constant sentries'. Most of these men seem to have been foremast hands. And many of the foremast men appear to have stuck with the captain in the mutiny.

At least one sentry had no stomach for the duty. John Prime was a 32-year-old ordinary seaman. He was born in Suffolk but had joined as part of the Port of London quota. In court he later complained that

I was to do no duty than that of Sentinel (saving) the getting up the Top Gallant Yards, and in with the Captain's barge . . . One time in particular when I came off my post at mid-day (being at three watches) I went to the galley to cook my dinner. I had not been there long 'ere Mr. Wrangham asked me, why I was not at work. I told him I had just come off sentry at twelve o'clock. He immediately took up one of the boatswain's mate's canes and he struck me with it. From this I went below to the master at arm's birth, considering the orders I had received from him as a protection from such violence. I would have gone to the quarterdeck, but from the treatment usually met with by shipmates I could have had but little hopes of redress from that quarter.

I had not long remained 'ere he (Mr Wrangham) visited me a second time, when he knocked me down with his fist. It was now Mr. Blair [the master-at-arms] remonstrated to him on the impropriety of his conduct. He replied he'd have me flogged and instantly complained of me to Mr. Hewitt, first lieutenant. When I was called aft . . . I related the transaction. Judge then how severe it was for me to here meet with treatment worse than before. Mr. Hewitt kicked me off, and said if it appeared again he would flog me.

I then went to work with the masters until seven or eight o'clock in the evening, and when the others were turning into their hammocks I was posted on the poop till midnight. Thus to stand sentinel at three watches and work when I was off like the others, who had no such duty: I considered [it] a grievance.

Notice that sentence: 'I would have gone to the quarter-deck, but from the treatment usually met with by shipmates I could have had but little hopes of redress from that quarter.' The men trusted neither Captain Home nor First Lieutenant Hewitt.

Note also that the sentries messed, worked and berthed with the other sailors. Marines and sailors had separate berths and separate jobs.

When the ship moored in Leith Roads the men hoped for shore leave: 'liberty'. The captains of the other ships in Leith Roads sent their men into Edinburgh in small groups of 20 or 30 at a time. The men were on their honour to return so that the next group could go ashore. The majority of naval ships did not allow such leave. But where it was tried it seems to have worked well. Sailors certainly thought it the only decent system.

Captain Home was not having it. His superiors blamed him for the many deserters. So he followed the more usual naval practice and forbade his men any shore leave. Then he followed another common practice. He had himself rowed into town by John Prime and his other bargemen. He slept ashore and left First Lieutenant Hewitt in charge of the ship.

The people of the *Defiance* got down to some serious angry drinking the next Saturday night.

At eight o'clock on Saturday night all seemed normal between decks to Master's Mate William Watson. He went on deck to take over as master of the watch on the *Defiance*. The first he knew of the mutiny was half an hour later. He was watching Acting Lieutenant Malcolm go down the starboard ladder into the waist. He saw Malcolm 'instantly seized and pulled down and took out of my sight aft under the half deck'. Then 'there was a general cry through the ship of "out all lights". The people were running in different directions through the ship.' They drove off the sentries on the gangway to the quarterdeck. The quarterdeck soon filled with 'armed people who came from different directions'.

Enthusiastic mutineers swept through below decks. If any man refused to rouse and join them, they cut down his hammock and spilled him on the deck. The lights were all out. At intervals men called out that they would have liberty and more grog. Mostly there was a 'profound silence'. It was broken only by the sound of cannon balls rolled along the deck to prevent officers moving around in the dark.

Watson went down to the wardroom to report the mutiny to First Lieutenant Hewitt. Hewitt went up to the main deck where

> I observed the people to be very noisy and riotous
> between decks. I immediately enquired amongst
> them the cause of the tumult and uproar which then
> prevailed. Some of them made answers. 'They
> wanted liberty and better usage, and liberty they
> would have.' I begged them to be peaceable and
> quiet and go to their hammocks. And that as soon as
> ever day light appeared in the morning I would hoist
> out one of the Cutters and send Mr. Hughes the fifth
> lieutenant with a letter to Sir George Home,
> requesting he would indulge them leave to go ashore
> twenty or thirty at a time, as he thought proper. It
> had very little weight with them. For they were
> determined to go on shore that night and some of
> them called 'All hands out boats'.

Hewitt found he 'could not prevail on them to desist from their intentions'. He scuttled up the main hatchway. Somebody threw a cannon ball up the hatchway after him.

On the quarterdeck Hewitt found a group of loyal men. Quietly, he ordered them to cut the tackle of the ship's boats to stop the mutineers from getting them into the water. Hewitt sent the clerk and three petty officers into the jolly boat. They rowed silently into the night to find Admiral Pringle on the *Asia* and beg for help.

On the gun deck the people were hauling out the starboard foremast gun. They pointed it aft. There was powder in the pan and shot in the barrel. Somebody stuck a crowbar down the mouth of the gun. If the officers tried to charge, the crowbar would whip through them.

It appeared to Hewitt that the mutineers 'were now in complete possession of the ship'. Watson, the master's mate, had other ideas. He quietly began to unship the quarterdeck guns. He wanted to point them aft so they could fire into the mutineers. Robert McLawrin saw him.

McLawrin was a local man, born in Edinburgh, who had shipped as part of the Sunderland quota. He was a skilled able seaman, and did duty as captain of the afterguard. To Watson he seemed to be 'one of the leaders of the mutineers'. According to Watson, McLawrin

stopped at the gangway and called to others '*to come up for they were casting the quarter deck guns loose*'. He with a number more came up and surrounded me and asked who gave me orders to cast the guns loose. I answered him, I had orders for what I was doing. Some of them laid hold of men and dragged me away from them: [McLawrin] telling me that I had no business with the guns.

McLawrin and some of the others went to cast the boats loose. They wanted to row for shore and probably never return. The tackle was cut and they could not leave.

By now it was ten o'clock at night. Hewitt was back below decks endeavouring

> to prevail on them to return to their duty and go peaceably and quietly to their hammocks. While I was speaking to them, I received a blow on the shoulder with a handspike, which nearly I believe beat off half the sleeve of my coat and bruised my shoulder . . .
>
> I asked them if they meant to murder. Some of them answered that not a hair of my head should be hurt and made enquiry amongst themselves who it was that struck me. But that was not discovered. I thought it not safe to trust myself any longer amongst them and immediately went off the quarter deck.
>
> By this time Admiral Pringle had made a signal for all boats manned and armed to come to our assistance. And when the people found that, they hauled the lower deck pots up; shotted the lower deck guns and run them out; with a full determination to sink every boat that should attempt to come alongside. The Jupiter's boat with a lieutenant in her came alongside. The officer came into the ship. The boat was obliged to put off immediately for fear of the people's being knocked on the head, by the shot that was thrown into her from the lower gun deck ports . . . Pistols were at this time fired out of the ports, but I don't know whether shotted or not, in order to intimidate the boats from coming alongside. The boats played round the ship. And as they either went ahead or astern, so the people assembled either on the poop or

the forecastle to keep them off.

Midshipman Robert Jones was in charge of one of the circling boats. From the poop McLawrin shouted at him 'Keep off, you bugger, keep off.' He turned tail and returned to his ship. Hewitt considered the balance of forces. He ordered his men to tell the boats to keep off too.

Hewitt may have been shaken by the adventures of Lieutenant James Dunbar, the officer who leapt aboard from the *Jupiter*'s boat:

> On my coming quite close I was repeatedly told to keep off. And on my ascending the side after having got on board, some person or persons on the gangway showed some opposition. The person most forward appeared so diminutive that I got on board without any resistance. When I got on the quarterdeck . . . There were assembled a number of men apparently inoffensive.

A few minutes later Lieutenant Dunbar was in the waist of the ship:

> Some men came by the larboard gangway and began relating their complaints. I recommended their going quietly below and await the result of the next day, or until their captain came. A voice unknown seemed to be displeased with my conduct or person. It is proper to observe that the greater part of the ship's company were in a state of drunkenness and as if they were recovering from their inebriety.
>
> At this time the other boats of the squadron were approaching the *Defiance*, rowing up in her wake principally. And the mutinous part of the ship's company ordered them to keep off or they would fire

into them. About this time a number of men armed with pikes came upon the quarterdeck from the larboard gangway, whether with any personal intention towards an attack on my life I know not. But not caring to risk the issue [and] judging any resistance imprudent, I retired hastily upon the poop being close pursued by the mutineers.

According to the surprised witness on the quarterdeck, they saw about a dozen men chasing Dunbar. They were variously armed with pikes, cutlasses and tomahawks. One enraged sailor was armed with the cook's burgoo stirrer. As Dunbar ran up the ladder to the poop, he slipped. He fell back almost into the arms of men behind him. But let Dunbar tell his own story:

I ran over the taff rail. Still pursued by the boarding pikes, I descended precipitately down the stern ladder. I was discovered in that situation, and a voice exclaimed 'There is a bugger on the stern ladder'. All boats at this time were out of reach and I thought of nothing but my own preservation. Some of the well disposed at that time in the Wardroom threw open the windows.

Some loyalists and officers had instinctively taken refuge on the quarterdeck. Others had headed for the wardroom: the officers' mess. Here were gathered a few officers and many of the foremast hands who had stood constant sentry duty. The rear window of the wardroom opened over the rudder. They gave Dunbar

such relief that I was enabled to get down the rudder and secret myself on it close under the coat. At this time I may observe, for so it struck me at the moment, that I was the object of their revenge.

I remained there for some time but I am not clear how long. About this time, several things and, I believe pikes amongst others, were thrown from the taffrail directly down. But I considered myself in greater security than elsewhere. In the meantime a firing was kept up on the boats. And assisted by a rope from the wardroom windows and at the pressing and urgent entreaties of those above me in the windows, and having no further means of retreat, I put the end of a rope with a knot under my arms. And was hauled by it up into the wardroom window, where I met with friendly reception from those who had assisted me in such situation. There I remained a considerable time during which I only heard from vague reports the state of the ship.

Below decks both sides had moved to gain control of the magazine. Matthew Hollister was the gunner's yeoman: the man in charge of the storeroom outside the powder magazine in the bottom of the ship. Hollister was 42 years old and a Londoner. He was an experienced sailor who had joined as part of the Chester quota. At the beginning of the mutiny Hollister was asleep in his hammock.

He was awoken by Gunner's Mate William Hyndson. Hyndson told Hollister that the ship was in a state of mutiny and he had the keys to the storeroom. They went there together. Hyndson gathered up some pole axes and slow matches. He took them up to the quarterdeck to arm the officers.

Shortly afterwards the outer door was shattered. Three men spilled into the storeroom, where Hollister still stood. Michael Cox was a 40-year-old ordinary seaman from London. John Lawson was an American from New York, 32 years old and an able seaman. William Morrison an ordinary seaman from Clerkenwell in London, was only 20. All three were much in liquor, but Lawson was the drunkest of the lot. They were after arms and powder for the mutineers.

Young Morrison asked Hollister for powder. Hollister said he had no powder: it was all in the inner storeroom. Between them and the powder was a stout door. It was always securely locked. Every experienced sailor knew one spark in the gunpowder magazine could blow up the whole ship. It had happened before.

In the 1790s people lacked our easy familiarity with great explosions. They were a new horror. At the Battle of the Nile in 1798 the French L'Orient of 120-guns exploded. For a few minutes the battle stopped. Nobody spoke. The guns were still. Men and women on both sides just looked.[8]

The Navy was careful with its powder. There was no light in the powder room itself. The yeoman of the powder room worked by the light from a lantern outside the storeroom, on the other side of a thick screen. The women and boys who fetched the powder had to wear cloth wrappings around their shoes, lest static electricity blow the ship sky high.

Now Matt Hollister and the yeoman of the powder room faced three drunks with naked candles. The drunks wanted to take their candles into the powder room. Hollister and the yeoman both said they didn't have the keys to the inner room. The yeoman opened an arms chest to show it was empty of powder. Young Morrison took some pole axes, tomahawks and gun wads out of the arms chest. Morrison told Hollister that if there were no keys he was going to break the door down. He then went to work on the inner door with a crowbar.

At that point Lieutenant Hughes came below. All three

men raced after him to see what was happening. A few minutes later William Parker took up a position in front of the magazine. He had a cutlass in one hand and a pistol in the other.

Parker was an experienced able seaman. He was 'captain of the maintop', and, at 24, young for the job. He originally came from Scarborough on the Yorkshire coast, but had joined the ship in London. He was a leader of the mutiny from the start. At 9:00 p.m. he was carrying a cutlass and directing his mates to point the guns aft. At 9:30 p.m. he was one of the leaders of the men trying to get the boats out. Some time around 10:00 p.m. he realized what was happening in the magazine. He did not want to be blown up. He went to stand guard.

Robert McLawrin came up to Parker. McLawrin had already led the men on to the quarterdeck. Now he wanted into the magazine. Parker barred his way. McLawrin hit Parker across the mouth twice.

'If you strike me again I will give you the contents of this pistol,' said Parker. 'You do not know the consequence of going into the magazine with lights. It's only that you're in liquor, or you would not attempt such a thing, to end the lives of the ship's company or the ship.'

McLawrin slunk away. The three men who had first broken open the magazine were feeling their drink. Matt Hollister saw Lawson standing outside the magazine: 'He seemed very much in liquor. Very ill. He was standing like a statue and as white as a sheet.' Young Morrison returned to his hammock briefly about midnight. He had 'shitted his trousers' and had to change. All three men were asleep by early morning. Parker remained on guard all night. When any attempted to pass he said, 'Take care, gentlemen, of what you are doing. Before any man shall go down with a

144

naked light, either they or me shall suffer death.'

Not all the people of the *Defiance* were part of the mutiny. Many were resting in their hammocks or hiding in corners. William Kiddy was one of the foremast men. When the mutiny began he took his wife and child forward to the manger. They waited out the night with the sheep. When the muster was called at noon on Sunday Kiddy went on deck.

Another man was brewing a pot of tea in the galley for his mother when the mutiny began. It took him half an hour to make the tea. He took it down to her. She slept that night in his hammock. He sat by her until morning, except for one trip on deck to make water.

The ship was full of women. Many of them had previous experience of drunken sailors in a mean mood. There were a large number of very drunken men running around the ship shouting and flourishing their tomahawks. Many of the women took refuge aft by the steward's room.

The mutiny was *disorganized*. The chaos around the magazine shows this clearly. The magazine was crucial. The mutineers needed gunpowder: otherwise they couldn't fight off the other ships in the fleet. But there was no immediate attack on the magazine. Instead there were three easily distracted drunks with naked candles. William Parker had been one of the leaders of the mutiny, a part that must have come naturally to him. As captain of the maintop he was perhaps the most skilled and respected of the able seamen. His leadership in daily work probably led easily to leadership in the mutiny. But when Parker saw what was happening around the magazine he stopped being a mutineer and became a sentry. In a properly organized mutiny, Parker would have detailed men to stand watch over the magazine. Then he would have begun to take out arms and powder carefully and gently.

Almost all mutinies were carefully planned beforehand. For one thing, any rebellion on a ship with a full complement of marines did not stand a chance without detailed organization. Even when Captain Pigot ordered the Hermiones to throw the lubbers overboard, the men waited two nights to organize the mutiny properly. No matter what the provocation, sailors did not simply riot.

The *Defiance* seems to be an exception. On the *Culloden* the majority of the ship's company had served together for 18 months. All the leaders of the mutiny had been on board for this period. They had survived a long cruise to the West Indies. They had come back with men dropping every day and 122 men in the sick bay. They had been through battle together at the 'Glorious First of June'. They had seen captains come and go. They were a unit, a 'ship's company'.

The people of the *Defiance* hardly knew each other. Most had been on board three months. Desertion was rife. They had seen no battles and only one short cruise. There was no informal lived solidarity from which organization could grow.

After midnight the ship began to settle down. Lieutenant Hughes wandered around. He made sporadic efforts to persuade little groups of men to return to their duty. At about two in the morning Captain Home finally returned on board. Two other captains joined him. The admiral had sent them to find out the men's grievances and, if possible, shut them up. All three captains went below to talk to the men. Some of the people told them they wanted liberty to go on shore; Home kept them on board like convicts, they said. Others insisted on no more five-water grog. Some emphasized that they wanted no more Captain Home, either.

At about this time some people broke into the spirit

stores. By five in the morning most people were asleep. Two of the captains went back to report to the admiral, leaving a forlorn Captain Home on the quarterdeck.

When morning came it was clear the people were still in control. The two captains returned to try to talk the men back to work. Below decks one of the mutineers began to beat the drum. The drum roll ws the 'call to quarters'. The people sprang to their stations by the guns. The ports went up and the guns rolled out. The sailors were at their quarters, ready for battle. But this time it was done at their own command. They were telling the captains something. They controlled the ship. They would fight any attempt to take it.

William Handy had been patrolling the deck since early morning. Handy was a 28-year-old Londoner. When he was pressed in Rochester on the Kent coast he rated himself a landsman, although he seems to have been an experienced sailor. He did duty as 'captain of the mast'. Now he was doing the same job for the mutineers. He paced back and forth along the deck. Sometimes a man popped up on to the deck hoping to join the loyalists on the quarterdeck. Handy ordered the man below. In his hand he held the cook's burgoo stirrer. Six hundred men ate a lot of burgoo porridge: the burgoo stirrer was a stout piece of wood, shaped like an oar but somewhat smaller.

When the drums began to roll Handy led a party of mutineers on to the quarterdeck. Handy carried his stirrer and the others held cutlasses. They ordered the loyalists to go below and man the guns with the others. Some seamen demurred. Handy had to thwack one man with the stirrer before he would go below. Another man was punched in the head and knocked down. But with a little gentle herding and some violent oaths, most loyalists went below. The officers were left on the quarterdeck with a few stragglers.

The captains had to negotiate. The two visiting captains went round the ship talking. They promised to convey the people's grievances to the admiral. They promised to take a letter from the ship's company to the admiral. It is unclear what else they promised. They persuaded the men to report for muster. The boatswain's pipes sounded at noon. The crew fell in for muster. After the muster Home put eight men into irons as ringleaders.

William Parker, the sentry at the magazine, was one of the eight. Robert McLawrin was another. He had led the attack on the quarterdeck on Saturday night, and a little later had hit Parker in the mouth. With them was William Handy, now without his burgoo stirrer.

The eight prisoners were on the quarterdeck as far aft as possible. Each man had chains around each ankle. A straight bar of iron was slotted through a ring on each chain. The prisoners therefore sat in a row, threaded along the bar like beads. Somebody rigged an awning to protect them from the sun.

The loyalists and the officers stood forward of the prisoners. They looked down upon the people in the waist and barred the way to the prisoners. The atmosphere was uneasy. Home ordered the men to run in the guns. Nobody obeyed. The officers held the quarterdeck and little else.

Somebody wrote out a letter for the captain to take to the admiral:

We the Ships Company belonging to His Majesty's Ship Defiance are sorry to trouble you with our present grievances which are stated as follows ———
We are sorry to inform You that being Commanded by Sir George Home who makes our

Case quite disagreeable to us, we are allowed a proportion of Rum of one half pint per day, that he pleases to have mixed for us with a proportion of five Waters, which renders our Grog of no service to us being thereby spoiled. in the 2nd. Place there are Cheese on board unfit for mens use and not of the quality allowed by the Navy, for that we have looked for redress, but being answered by our Captain. Who gave us Priviledge to be a Judge of Provisions. Allowing that we/as we must suppose/ were no Judges of Provisions, 3d. We have then on board an Acting Lieutenant. Mr. Markam who when he gets intoxicated uses us in the most brutal manner, by striking and abusing us unbecoming to human beings, 4th we have no Liberty granted us which all the ships here has Liberty, but us just the same as Prisoners their 7 of our Men in Irons, which they being intoxicated in liquor and they were more taken notice of than any of the Rest, and we hope that You will look over Them, it will be a bad Consequence to go to Sea with Ship without redress.

Defiance Ships Company.[9]

The letter was probably written by John Graham, the same landsman who had copied the ship's log for Midshipman Mudie. Graham had joined as part of the quota for Whitby in North Yorkshire. Yorkshire speech, then and now, mostly leaves out the word 'the'. That's why Graham wrote 'with Ship without Redress', instead of 'with the Ship without Redress'. 'We hope that You will look over Them' means 'We hope you will overlook them.' At the end of the letter there was a quiet threat: if the ship put to sea without redress the people would act. Perhaps they would mutiny.

Perhaps they would run for the coast of France.

At about three in the afternoon the two captains went back to the admiral's flagship. They took the letter with them. As he left, Captain Latchmere told Captain Home he would have to release the prisoners before dark. If he did not, the men would release themselves.

As the afternoon wore on the people began to form groups in the waist. (The waist was the open deck below the quarterdeck.) There was a general murmuring. The officers could hear constant loud shouting, but few individual voices were clear. Foremastman John Prime was still angry about being a constant sentry and working three watches. He kept popping up to shout that he would do no more duty as a sentry. Some voices shouted that they should all go aft to free the prisoners. Others repeated the original demands: 'Liberty and no five-water grog.' Below decks there was constant cheering and the rumble of cannon balls rolled along the deck.

At six dusk was closing in. The officers sensed movements in the waist to rush the deck. They would soon be defenceless in the dark and unable to tell mutineer from loyalist. There were scores of loyal men on the quarterdeck. Captain Home ordered them to take up arms to subdue the people.

Nobody obeyed.

The loyalists may have felt frightened and outnumbered. They may have been unwilling to kill their mates. Probably it was a bit of both. Captain Home ran up a signal to the other ships in the squadron asking for assistance. The flagship did not reply. No boats came. Home did what he had to do. He ordered Lieutenant Hewitt to release the men in irons. First Home retired from the quarterdeck to sulk in his cabin, leaving the public humiliation to Hewitt.

Hewitt ordered the men released. He said to William Parker, 'as you are now at liberty once more, I hope that you will take care and behave yourself better in future'.

'You may depend on it,' replied the happy Parker.

Hewitt took another prisoner by the arm and led him to the gangway to the forecastle. In full view of the ship's company he said, 'You have got your liberty. Avoid such things in future and return to your duty. Behave well and no more will be thought of it.'

Then the lieutenant turned to the ship's company below him, saying, 'Now, my lads, you have got your prisoners. Return to your duty. Go below to your hammocks, and no more will be thought of it.'

Some of the crowd in the waist were still shouting. They refused to believe the prisoners had all been freed. Hewitt repeated his promise that there would be no further trouble. He said they could come up on the quarterdeck and look for themselves if they wanted.

The people realized they had won. They gave three cheers and returned happily to their duties. But they still expected a reply to their letter from the admiral. What the people did not know was that Lieutenant Hewitt had no intention of keeping his promise.

Admiral Pringle read the men's letter. He was not sure what to do. Luckily the *Calcutta* was part of his squadron. Admiral Pringle could turn for advice to the *Calcutta*'s brave and decisive captain. And Captain William Bligh already had some previous experience with mutineers.

# 9

## 'How came he to sleep in your hammock with you that night?'

Admiral Pringle called his captains to a council of war. William Bligh was there and advised his fellow officers:

> Many plans were mentioned, & the best way discussed, how to subdue this mutiny, & I did not hesitate to declare that a party of troops embarked on board of another ship & laid alongside, was the most effectual manner that I knew of, because they would be protected, which by any other means they would not if resistance was made.[1]

Pringle took Bligh's advice. As he had no marines and could not get any soldiers on short notice, he borrowed 200 'fencibles'. The fencibles were a part-time home-guard force under the control of the Navy. Many of them were seamen and fishermen who had joined as a protection against the press gang. There had been several recent mutinies by fencibles and the militia. Pringle could not really trust them, but they were all he had.[2]

He put them on board two 74-gun ships, the *Jupiter* and the *Edgar*, ordering both ships to weigh anchor and put themselves alongside the *Defiance*. At the last minute the admiral changed his mind. He had his reasons.

John Nicol was one of the seamen on the *Edgar* that day. He recorded:

While we lay in Leith Roads, a mutiny broke out in the Defiance, 74; the cause was, their captain gave them five-water grog; now the common thing is three-waters. The weather was cold; the spirit thus reduced was, as the mutineers called it, as thin as muslin, and quite unfit to keep out the cold. No seaman could endure this in cold climates. Had they been in hot latitudes they would have been happy to get it thus, for the sake of the water; but then they would not have got it. The Edgar was ordered alongside the Defiance, to engage her, if necessary, to bring her to order . . . She was manned principally by fishermen, stout resolute dogs. When bearing down upon her, my heart felt so sad and heavy, not that I feared death or wounds, but to fight my brother, as it were, I do not believe the Edgar's crew would have manned the guns. They thought the Defiance men were in the right; and had they engaged us heartily, as we would have done a French 74, we would have done no good, only blown each other out of the water, for the ships were of equal force; and if there was any odds, the Defiance had it in point of crew.[3]

Pringle ordered Captain Bligh to take 80 men in open boats and seize the *Defiance*. Bligh didn't like it: the boats were too vulnerable. However, we can guess at the admiral's point of view. If the Edgars and Jupiters refused to fight Pringle faced a fleet mutiny. If they fought he would lose hundreds of men and might lose three ships into the bargain. In 1795 food riots, strikes and monster demonstrations were blazing across Britain.[4] If the *Defiance* won the battle the victorious broadsides would be heard by every angry democrat and hungry mother in the country. If Bligh and his men were blown to smithereens that would be a most unfortunate tragedy. But the Royal Navy could live with it.

On the *Defiance* one of the mutineers was already a prisoner. John Prime was still angry about standing sentry duty and working three shifts. At eight o'clock Monday morning Corporal Bradly reported to Lieutenant Hewitt that Prime was still refusing to be a sentry. Hewitt ordered the corporal to bring Prime aft to the quarterdeck:

> I then asked him if he had refused the corporal to stand sentinel. He, John Prime, said that he had, and that he would not be a soldier. I ordered him my-self to stand sentinel. He told me he positively would not. On which I ordered him on the poop under the charge of the sentinel there.

A little later Leonard Bearby and Martin Ealey were working in the head. Martin Ealey was 27, an Irish able seaman. Born in Waterford, he had joined as part of the London quota. Saturday night Ealey had been among those driving the skulkers forward. Bearby, a foremast man, had refused to leave his berth. Ealey was very much in liquor and had beaten Bearby brutally. On Sunday, Ealey had been one of the eight men released from irons. At some point during that day Bearby had gone on to the quarterdeck and told the captain about the beating.

Now Bearby was washing the swabs in the head and Ealey was wringing them out. Ealey told Bearby 'What a bad fellow I was for offering to swear against him and take his life away and all that. And I told him I would not wish to take his life away and made an offer to him of half a guinea.'

Bearby was scared. He hoped to buy off Ealey's anger with two weeks' wages. Ealey refused the money.

A bit before noon the men of the *Defiance* could see the boats coming. Somebody threw a letter on to the quarterdeck.

> We, the Ships Co. of H.M. Ship Defiance under your comd. (all and Singular) make bold to inform you, that we are not agreeable that any Marines shall come on board, till we have an answer from the Admiralty, and then we will with the greatest Pleasure comply with any terms conformable to the Rules of His Majesty's Navy, and furthermore we are agreeable to do the duty of Marines until this affair is settled, and till then, never a man shall go out or come into the Ship, except Officers or Commanders ——
> 2nd. There is a quantity of Men upon record who gave in their Names to the Ships Clerk Mr. Thompson as Royalists, these we ordain to get out of the Ship (to make room for Marines as soon as we have convenience to receive them) and no other. Give in under our hands this 19th day of Oct. 1795, Your Humble Servants and dutifull Ships Company upon Honble [i.e. honourable] Terms.[5]

The gloves are off. The scabs are described as 'Royalists'. The opposite of a royalist was a republican. In Britain in 1795, to be a republican was to be a revolutionary.

The letter is proud, angry, arrogant. The people 'make bold', they 'ordain'. The writer, as before, is John Graham. He writes in the tone and style of a nobleman addressing an inferior. The militants were feeling their power.

They were also bluffing. The letters from the Windsor Castles and the Cullodens are polite, clear and firm. They didn't need loud words: their organization and their guns spoke for them. But no Defiance, mutineer or officer, knew what would happen as the boats approached.

John Sullivan started climbing the rigging. Saturday night he had chased Lieutenant Dunbar over the poop with a boarding pike in his hand. At two on Sunday morning he had come on to the starboard gangway and called, 'Let us go down and break the spirit room open for we will have grog'. Sunday he had been in and out of irons. He did his regular duty in the tops. Now he was climbing up to his working home, hoping to stay out of sight. A lieutenant saw him and shouted at him to come down. Sullivan descended sheepishly and stood quietly on the deck.

The boats came alongside. There was a 'great noise below'. From the waist and the lower decks hundreds of voices roared, 'Keep off, keep off, we'll sink you'. On the quarterdeck the master and the officers began to cast off the guns.

Bligh later wrote about those moments:

With these two boats I proceeded in two Divisions until close to the Ship. When from the orders I had given the respective officers, the Divisions opened and rowed to each Gangway and preceded by myself & a Major, the Commanding officer of the Soldiers in a separate Boat. Instantly was the cry of one & all – 'clear away the Guns – sink them', and we cheered the troops not to mind this, but to come on, which they did, and got up on the Poop without any hurt but a slight Bruise or two & a boat stove with the shot that were thrown out of the ports. We had now the remaining soldiers to get on board, which I effected very speedily and without any resistance

156

which it was expected I should have met with, both
in going out and coming in: but I had only a few
fellows who pointed at me and said there he goes.

The sailors had heard about Bligh. They may have used
other words besides 'there he goes'.[6]

The mutiny was broken. Captain Home emerged from
the shadows to reclaim effective command from Lieutenant
Hewitt. He clapped the eight men back in irons. The
questioning began. Soon 17 men were in irons. Admiral
Pringle had them transferred to the locked room on one of
the press tenders. This was unusual. He may not have trusted
the crews of his other 74s.

Pringle was certainly nervous. He wrote to the Admiralty
that the *Defiance* was quiet. But though the fencibles 'have
gone upon their service with alacrity,' he said he would be
happier with real soldiers on board. Indeed, he thought that
essential to keep control of the ship.[7]

Three days later Pringle finally got hold of his soldiers:
135 officers and men of the 134th Regiment replaced the
fencibles. However, he still had no marines on any of his
ships and could find only a handful of soldiers to do sentry
duty on his flagship. He wrote to the Admiralty:

It is impossible for me to stir from that ship [the
*Defiance*] or carry her to sea on a cruise, as I cannot
esteem her in safety till She is in some of His Majesty's
Ports, and indeed it appears highly advisable to me that
Her present Crew should be turned over into other ships.[8]

So Pringle sailed his whole squadron 400 miles down the
coast to join the fleet at the Nore buoy in the Thames
estuary. A contingent of marines from Chatham came on
board the *Defiance*.[9]

Three months later, on 20 January 1796, the trial of the 17 mutineers began. William Bligh had received the signal to report to serve on the court martial. He objected. He wrote his admiral that he had been the principal officer in putting down the mutineers and had therefore seen the ship in a state of mutiny. He felt it was his duty to mention this fact for the information of the admiralty and 'in justice to the prisoners'. Bligh was released from court-martial duty.[10]

The trial lasted 22 days. Captain Home was a disorganized and incompetent prosecutor. There is no reason to believe that his 17 selected victims were the leaders of the mutiny. The crew had said firmly that the eight men first clapped in irons were no more guilty than the rest. They were just drunk and the officers had noticed them more. But these eight men did conduct a joint defence. They asked the court to delay the case until their attorney arrived. The court said they would hear the prosecution witnesses immediately. They would wait for the attorney before hearing the defense.

The attorney drew up a joint-written defence for all eight men. He argued that Hewitt had promised forgiveness when he released them from irons. Robert McLawrin, Martin Ealey and John McDonald signed the defence with their names. William Parker, George Wythick, William Froud, John Sullivan and William Handy signed with their marks.

Each of the eight defendants called Lieutenant Hewitt as a witness. Each asked him identical questions. Under pressure an embarrassed Hewitt admitted that he had publicly promised an amnesty. But he added that he had done so under duress and had had no intention of keeping his promise. The court, of course, did not care what Hewitt had promised. If the prisoners had done what they were accused of, then they were guilty.

Two of the 17 defendants were discharged 'not proven'.

Six cases were found 'proven in part'. Two were to be flogged round the fleet with 100 lashes. Four were sentenced to 300 lashes. One of them was John Graham, the letter-writer. They got him by comparing the mutineers' letters with the journal he had written up for Mudie as the ship sailed into the Firth of Forth. John Prime got 300 lashes for refusing sentry duty. So did William Parker, who had spent the long night guarding the magazine and threatening death to any mutineer attempting to pass.

On 11 February the court sentenced nine men to death. On the twentieth Prime, Graham and Froud were flogged round the fleet. On 6 March an extra 45 marines came on board the *Defiance*. That evening the nine prisoners came on board. Two days later, in the morning, they were brought on deck. One of them was John Lawson, the drunken American who had broken into the magazine. Another was William Handy, who had patrolled the deck with the cook's burgoo stirrer.

At 9:00 a.m. five men were hanged. Robert McLawrin was the man who slapped Parker in the face outside the magazine. William Morrison and Michael Cox had tried to force the magazine open. Morrison was so drunk that first night that he shitted his trousers. He was 20. Martin Ealey was the man who refused the half-guinea when he'd been working with Bearby in the head. John Sullivan was the man who had tried to disappear into the rigging as Bligh approached.[11]

Next day the captain had all hands turned up. He made a speech to them. But the Admiralty was still frightened of the *Defiance*. They dispersed the crew. One hundred men went to the *Director*, now commanded by William Bligh. Within a month almost all the rest of the seamen had been transferred to other ships,[12] although many petty officers remained on the *Defiance*.

The mutiny on the *Defiance* was a defeat. The men lost because they were disorganized. The crucial moment was when Bligh came alongside. They lacked the collective organization to turn their shouts into actions. Their fate shows clearly why all other mutinies were carefully planned beforehand.

But the Defiance men were not broken. Even after the executions the Navy did not dare let them remain together. And at the court martial some of the witnesses showed a spirit of decency and resistance.

'Big Job' Else testified over and over again against his shipmates. Jacob Hill, a foremast man, told the court what he thought of men like Else:

> On Monday morning after the prisoners were in irons, I was warming some water on the galley fire on the larboard side and Job Else came in to warm some water in a pot the same. I was standing just close by the prop by the bar, and some other people were there, I don't know who. I said to Job Else, 'What, have you got Martin Ealey in irons? I understand he's in irons.' And he made answer and said yes. Then I said, 'Job, what did he do to you? Did he knock you down?' He said he did not knock him down but he pulled him and lugged him about a great deal and used him very ill. And I answered, 'What's that all he has done to you. And the poor man has got in chains, and I saw him quietly at different times.'
>
> He then made answer that he should not have thought so much of it. But Martin Ealey was the man who went and made a complaint to the doctor when he (Else) was in the doctor's list. That he went

and told the doctor he was fighting in the galley
with one of the maintop men. And I said to him,
'Why, that's a very hard thing that a man should
lose his life through such a thing as that.'

Joseph Nicholson was a witness for the defence of John
Lawson, the American. His evidence gives a vivid picture of
life below decks at the start of the mutiny. Nicholson and
Lawson were probably lovers. Nicholson is trying to save his
mate's life. He is establishing that Lawson was so drunk at
the start of the mutiny that he could not have been a
ringleader and was not responsible for his actions. Lawson
was pardoned, and Nicholson's evidence probably saved his
life. Notice that at the end of his evidence Nicholson gets so
angry he takes the great risk of using sarcasm to the judges.

Lawson: On the evening of 17th October last did I turn into
    your hammock and ask what time was it?
Nicholson: The prisoner Lawson did turn into my hammock
    about seven o-clock that evening.
Lawson: What was the time and occasion of my turning out
    of it again?
Nicholson: The occasion was that they were cutting the
    hammocks down,when the prisoner said to me, we had
    better turn out. This might be about ten o-clock . . .
The court asked: Did the prisoner and you always sleep
    together or had you separate hammocks?
Nicholson: No. We had separate hammocks, but he laid
    alongside of me.
The court: How came he to sleep in your hammock with you
    that night?
Nicholson: I supposed he was a little intoxicated with liquor
    when he turned in.

The court: How did you so particularly notice the time of his turning into your hammock and the time of his turning out again?

Nicholson: One of my messmates had a watch and looked at it when we turned out and there was a light in the berth.

The court: Who turned first into the hammock?

Nicholson: The prisoner turned in just before me.

The court: How came you then not to turn into his hammock?

Nicholson: It was not hung up.

The court: How came you to have a candle in your berth at ten o-clock at night?

Nicholson: There was a woman and child laying there at the time and it happened that the child was frightened at the noise and she was looking at it.

The court: Did you wake your messmate to look at his watch?

Nicholson: No. He was awake in the berth.

The court: What could be your reason for wishing to know the time so exactly?

Nicholson: My reason was that I supposed I should be called on as a witness for John Lawson.

The court: What reason had you to suppose you should be called on as a witness for John Lawson?

Nicholson: In case he should happen to be detected afterwards, that I might know the time.

I have concentrated on the *Culloden* and the *Defiance* because those mutinies were followed by long courts martial. Therefore we know more about what happened on those ships. We know almost nothing about what happened on the *Windsor Castle* because the men won a full pardon. We know more about defeats. This does not mean that they were more important than victories.

162

Let's take the big mutinies in the order they happened. At the beginning of the war in 1793, the Winchelseas wrote a letter and held a demonstration. They had two men flogged round the fleet and the Admiralty agreed to remove their captain. Next year, in 1794, the Windsor Castles took over their ship in the Mediterranean. They ran out the guns. They were ready to fight unless they got rid of their captain and gained an amnesty. The admiral gave in.

Within weeks the Cullodens at Spithead refused to put to sea. The admiral on the spot was reluctant to take them on. The Admiralty, while prepared to promise a refit, feared that another amnesty would lead to a rash of mutinies. So Pakenham promised forgiveness and the Admiralty prosecuted.

Next year, 1795, the same thing happened on the *Defiance*. Lieutenant Hewitt promised forgiveness and a trial followed. The Admiralty was angry with Captain Home for releasing the men from irons on Sunday night. They were pleased with Admiral Pringle's resolute action in putting down the mutiny.

In September 1795 there was a mutiny on the *Terrible* in the Mediterranean. The Terribles were angry with their captain and with the rotten bread he forced them to eat. The *Windsor Castle* was part of the Mediterranean fleet. The Terribles also seized the lower decks and barricaded themselves in. Captain Campbell shouted, 'We'll have no Windsor Castles here.' He had the marines take a crowbar to the planks of the deck and begin firing down into the men. Several were badly wounded. A few were flogged on the spot until they broke down and talked. After the court martial, the 'ringleaders' were hanged. The whole fleet, including the *Windsor Castle*, was forced to watch the execution.

Debt, want and the press gang drove men into the Navy.

Corruption and the rope's end across their backs outraged them. Discontent was continuous. Murmuring and informal protests were common. Mutinies were rare. But the possibility of mutiny was always at the back of men's minds. The man-of-war was a pressure cooker. After the *Windsor Castle* the Admiralty closed the escape valves. Two years later the great fleet mutinies were to explode at Spithead and the Nore. But that is another story.

# 'Epilogue: A red flag at the mizzen topmast head'

The sequel to *The Cutlass and the Lash* will be a full account of the mutinies of 1797. But here I must touch briefly on some events of that year to complete the stories of the *Culloden* and the *Defiance*.

In April 1797 the remanned *Defiance* was swinging at anchor at Spithead, off Portsmouth. The ship was now part of the Channel Fleet, with a new captain and a new crew. But it was still the same old Navy. The sailors were angry. Soldiers had recently received a pay rise. So, too, had naval officers. But seamen had not received a pay rise for 150 years. The Channel Fleet was organizing. Each ship sent a petition to their former admiral, Black Dick Howe. Against orders, boats began to row from ship to ship. One carried a letter from the Royal Sovereigns to the people of the *Defense*:

> Friends,
>     I am happy to hear of your honourable courage
> towards redress. We are carrying on the business
> with the greatest expeditions. We flatter ourselves
> with the hopes that we shall obtain our wishes, for
> they had betters go to war with the whole globe than
> with their own subjects. We mean the day that the
> petitions go to London to take charge of the ships

until we have a proper answer from Government. The signal will be first made by the Queen Charlotte. The first signal is the Union Jack at the main with two guns fired: that is for taking charge and sending the officers and women out of every ship. The second signal is a red flag at the mizzen topmast head, and two guns: that is to send a speaker from every ship.[1]

It didn't work out quite that way. On 16 April 1797 Admiral Gardner ordered the fleet to sea. Ship by ship, they refused. Rowing pickets spread out through the fleet. Officers stood helplessly as sailors came up over the side and addressed each ship's company. Two delegates were elected from every ship to a committee of the fleet. The Spithead mutiny had begun.

The lords of the Admiralty raced down to Portsmouth to negotiate. Within a week their lordships offered pay rises of around 20 per cent. The committee of delegates met on the *Queen Charlotte*. They liked the offer.

Admiral Gardner went to meet the delegates. He was an admiral's admiral: bluff, tempestuous, joking, brave, open, foul-mouthed. He heartily congratulated the delegates on agreeing to the offer. The committee explained they had to wait for the return of four delegates from shore. Gardner accepted this. He sat down in the cabin among the delegates and began to write out a letter of thanks for the delegates to sign and send to the Admiralty.

Valentine Joyce was one of the four delegates still on shore. He was a 29-year-old quartermaster's mate on the *Royal Sovereign*. He was a skilled seaman, born on the seafaring island of Jersey.[2] But 'Valentine Joyce' is not a Jersey name: it is Catholic Irish. Before he joined the Navy

Joyce had run a tobacconist's shop in Belfast. In 1793 he was arrested for sedition and sent into the fleet as punishment. He was an active United Irishman. He was also the informal leader of the delegates and the fleet.

We do not know what Joyce and his three mates were doing in Portsmouth at this critical moment. Perhaps they were consulting with revolutionaries on shore. Perhaps they were getting pissed. They returned to the *Queen Charlotte* to find the other delegates gathered around Gardner. Joyce knew that once they signed the letter of thanks they were all dead men. He began arguing with the delegates that they must have a signed pardon from the king before they returned to duty.

Many delegates did not agree. Joyce walked out of the cabin on to the quarterdeck. He and his three mates started talking to the Charlottes on the forecastle and in the waist. 'Remember the *Culloden*,' they said. 'Remember the *Culloden*.'

The Charlottes remembered. The *Culloden* was now in the Mediterranean, but two years before had been part of the Channel Fleet. Every ship in the fleet had heard the execution gun. Pakenham had promised an amnesty and then betrayed the Cullodens. Pakenham was still a captain in the Channel Fleet.

The Charlottes surged aft on to the quarterdeck. Admiral Gardner saw which way the wind was blowing. 'You're a damned mutinous blackguard set that deserves hanging,' he screamed. He grabbed one man by the collar. 'I'll hang you, and I'll hang every fifth man in the fleet.'

The Charlottes bustled Admiral Gardner roughly off the ship. That afternoon the red flag flew from the *Royal George*, Valentine Joyce's ship. The delegates met there. They sent the Admiralty a message. They would return to

167

duty when they had a pardon signed by the king for every ship in the fleet. All around Spithead the sailors opened the ports and ran out the great guns.

Earl Spencer, First Lord of the Admiralty, left Portsmouth that night. By nine the next morning he was in London. At five in the afternoon he left London with Prime Minister William Pitt. Four hours later they were in Windsor Castle with King George III. The king signed a royal proclamation decreeing a total pardon. A hundred copies were printed and rushed south. By next morning every captain in the Channel Fleet read out the proclamation to a cheering ship's company.

Francis Watts, James Johnston, Cornelius Sullivan, Joseph Curtain and Jeremiah Collins: five Cullodens were dead. They were not forgotten.

The mutiny lasted three more weeks. The sailors won most of what they wanted on pay and conditions. They put ashore 114 unpleasant officers. Black Dick Howe came down and signed an agreement with the delegates. It was the biggest single victory by workers in Britain until the dockers' strike almost a century later, in 1889.

The fleet at the Nore had already mutinied before Spithead finished. The first ship at the Nore to mutiny and the last to go back was the *Director*, commanded by Captain William Bligh. The year before 100 men had been transferred from the *Defiance* to the *Director*.

Matthew Hollister was one of them. The muster book of the *Defiance* gives his birthplace as London and his age as 42. In the *Director*'s muster book he is 56 and Bristol born. It is the same Matt Hollister on both ships. Men were not too particular what they told the ship's clerk. All we know for certain is that Hollister was an old salt from southern England.[3]

Hollister held the same rank on both ships: gunner's yeoman. On the *Defiance* he had faced the three drunken mutineers who tried to break into the powder magazine. At the court martial he testified for the prosecution, when he had been careful to emphasize that the men were too drunk really to know what they were doing. His evidence helped to save William Parker's life. He seems not to have joined the disorganized mutiny on the *Defiance*. But we cannot be sure. We do know that he was the leader of the mutiny on the *Director*.

The sailors at the Nore sent four delegates to talk to the mutineers at Spithead. The four delegates arrived in Portsmouth the day after victory was finally won. Portsmouth was a carnival of the oppressed. Admirals and delegates marched together behind the massed bands of the fleet and the marines. Prostitutes and seamen huzza'd in the streets. The four delegates from the Nore approached Valentine Joyce. Matt Hollister was one of the four. The young revolutionary tobacconist from Belfast shook hands with the old Defiance.

# Glossary

Able Seaman: an experienced seaman, able to 'hand, reef and steer': pull on the ropes, work high up in the rigging, and take the wheel. Paid slightly more than an ordinary seaman.

Boatswain: the officer in charge of making the men sail the ship. Also in charge of sails, rigging and ship's boats. A disciplinarian, the 'bosun' was always a very skilled sailor promoted from the ranks.

Boatswain's mates: the boatswain's assistants. Spent much of their time harrying or beating men who would not work.

Bounty: the money paid to a man when he volunteered to join the Navy.

Captain: the man in charge. The officer in charge of a ship of any sort was addressed as captain, no matter what his rank. Thus Captain Bligh of the *Bounty* was in fact rated a lieutenant. A man who was a permanent captain was technically a Post Captain. The Captain of the Foretop would be the experienced sailor in charge of the foretopmen in one watch. Similarly, the Captain of the Mainmast was the sailor on each watch in charge of the men pulling on ropes in the area around the mainmast. The Captain of Marines was often a lieutenant. The man who cleaned the toilet was Captain of the Head.

Carpenter: the warrant officer in charge of maintenance and repairs to wood. On a completely wooden ship this was an important post. Under him were the 'carpenter's mates': under the 'carpenter's crew'.

Commodore: a Post Captain in charge of a squadron of two or more ships.

Cooper: in charge of making and repairing barrels. Therefore also in charge of opening stores and getting water.

Forecastle: the raised deck at the front of the ship. The sailors exercised and played here. They slept below the forecastle. By extension, the 'forecastle' was the sailors as a group.

Gunner: the warrant officer in charge of the guns, ammunition stores, and firing the guns. Usually promoted from the ranks, he had to be literate and competent in mathematics.

Gun Deck: the lower deck with the most guns on it. Sometimes called main deck.

Landsman: a sailor with no experience of the sea. Before 1797 paid at the same rate as ordinary seamen but usually recorded in the muster books as a separate rank. After 1797 paid slightly less than ordinary seamen.

Lieutenant: commissioned officers who held the 'king's commission', rather than just an Admiralty warrant. They had been midshipmen and hoped to be captains. They were supposed to serve seven years at sea and pass an examination before being commissioned. On each ship the lieutenant were ranked in strict order of seniority: the First Lieutenant was the one who had held a commission longest, the Second Lieutenant would have 'passed Lieutenant' a year or so after him, and so on.

Master: the warrant officer in charge of navigating the ship. Originally, the master had been the captain. The man called Captain was the military officer who led the men of the ship in battle with another ship. The master would be a professional sailor, the captain an officer and a gentleman, often very ignorant. By 1790 the captain was in charge of the whole ship and was usually a quite competent sailor. But the master still did the navigation and kept the log. In tricky sailing situations the captain and master often consulted together and sometimes quarrelled. A captain who ran his ship aground against his master's advice was in a very sticky situation. Today the distinction remains in the Merchant Navy: the boss is called the master, not the captain. Sometimes the master was promoted to become a commissioned officer. James Cook, for instance, started his career as an apprentice on coaling vessels and worked his way up to Post Captain by this route.

Master's mates: his assistants. Usually promoted sailors, but sometimes a captain shipped extra 'young gentlemen' as master's mates if he had used up all midshipman places and still had friends and relatives to oblige.

Master-at-arms: ships head policeman. In charge of all prisoners awaiting trial and flogging.

Midshipmen: junior officers. They usually had their own berth and mess in the middle of the ship. Some of them were 'young gentlemen' serving an apprenticeship before becoming lieutenants. Some were 'elderly mids': men without influence who would never be promoted, or skilled and reliable sailors promoted from the ranks.

Nore: the name of a buoy at the mouth of the Thames. By extension, 'the Nore' was the large fleet usually anchored in the Thames estuary.

Ordinary seaman: a sailor with some experience at sea, but not fully skilled. Paid slightly less than an 'able seaman'.

But since able seamen were more likely to be flogged for mistakes, many able seamen shipped as ordinary seamen.

People: the sailors, as in 'the people of the *Culloden*'. The officers are not included. This expression was used all the time by both officers and men.

Press: the forcible recruitment of men into the Navy. In most major ports there were 'press gangs' of a dozen or so permanently employed thugs under the command of a naval lieutenant. Cornwall had no press gangs because the Cornish were too fierce. A ship would also often send a gang of trusted sailors ashore under the command of an officer to grab men from the street. Naval ships also 'pressed' men off merchant ships.

Purser: the officer in charge of buying and distributing food, drink and cloth. He was a businessman in his own right, and the office of purser was bought and sold like a shop. It was widely assumed that all pursers were corrupt.

Quarters: battle stations.

Quarter-deck: the raised deck at the rear of the ship where the officers took exercise. Here the ship was steered, and here the captain stood. By extension, the 'quarter-deck' was the officers as a group.

Quarter-gunner: an experienced sailor who supervised the firing of several guns in battle.

Quarter-master: the petty officer in charge of the steering of the ship. There was usually one quarter-master on each 'watch': each shift. The quartermaster's mates usually did the actual manhandling of the wheel.

Quota-men: each borough and county was required to raise a certain number of men each year for the Navy. The local authorities paid various cash bounties to encourage men to sign up as part of their quota.

Run: deserted.

Spithead: wide, sheltered anchorage between Portsmouth and the Isle of Wight. The home of the Channel Fleet.

Surgeon: the ship's doctor, a warrant officer. His most important skill was doing amputations.

Tender: a boat which supplied the needs of a larger ship. A press tender carried pressed men from shore to the ships, and often travelled from port to port.

Waist: the area of the main deck, between and below the quarter-deck and the forecastle. The 'waisters' were the less skilled sailors stationed in the waist.

Ward Room: the mess and club-house for lieutenants and some warrant officers. Always aft. Sometimes called the gun-room, which is not the same thing as the gunners' berth.

# Notes

*All references to 'Adm.' in the notes refer to volumes in the Admiralty records, now in the Public Record Office, Ruskin Avenue, Kew, London.*

## Prologue: 'I have been a republican since the beginning of the war'

1. For the *Hermione* I have relied on Dudley Pope, *The Black Ship*, London: Weidenfeld & Nicolson, 1963. My emphasis varies from Pope's, but it is an excellent history.
2. It is not possible to be exact about numbers. The mutineers sensibly destroyed the relevant muster book.
3. This account is based on the court martial of the *Winchelsea* mutineers in Adm. 1:5330.
4. This letter is enclosed in a letter from Admiral Parker to the Admiralty, 17 September 1793, in Adm. 1:1005, Letter 480.
5. The ship's log, in Adm. 52:2539.
6. Captain Fisher asked the Admiralty to pardon them after that, since they had been punished enough. Letter from Fisher to Admiral Parker and Parker to Admiralty, 18 October 1793, in Adm. 1:1005, Letter 514.
7. Enclosure from Fisher to Parker in Parker to Admiralty, 21 September 1793, in Adm. 1:1005, Letter 485.
8. The ship's log, in Adm. 52:2539.

# 1. 'The crew, too, by some means had the impression that my mother had brought me on board to get rid of me'

1. Samuel Leech, *Thirty Years from Home, or a Voice from the Main Deck*, London: John Neale, 1844, pp.14-15.
2. Actually, a '74' usually carried more than 74 guns, but some of them did not really count. I am simplifying here.
3. A.T. Mahan, *The Influence of Sea Power upon the French Revolution and Empire, 1793-1812*, 2 volumes, London: Sampson, Low & Co., 1892, volume 1, p.139.
4. Dudley Pope, *Life in Nelson's Navy*, London: George Allen & Unwin, 1981, p.206; Michael A. Lewis, *A Social History of the Navy, 1793-1815*, London: George Allen & Unwin, 1960, pp.277-8.
5. Captain Marryat, *Suggestions for the Abolition of Impressment in the Naval Service*, London: J.M. Richardson, 1822, pp.25-34. This is the same Marryat who wrote *Midshipman Easy* and *The Children of the New Forest*.
6. John Bechervaise, *Thirty-Six Years of a Seafaring Life*, Portsea: 1839, pp.107-8.
7. We are fortunate in having quite a few memoirs of life below decks in these years. They present the Navy from a wide range of points of view. John Bechervaise was a quarter-master bred to the sea. James Durand was a very angry American pressed into service (James Durand, *An Able Seaman of 1812*, edited by George S. Brooks, New Haven: Yale University Press, 1926). 'Jack Nastyface' became a printer and used his press to relieve his hatred of the Navy in his *Nautical Economy, or Forecastle Recollections*, Cheapside: William Robinson, 1836. William Richardson was a gunner and a warrant officer for many years, but ever held fast to his contempt for admirals (William Richardson, *A Mariner of England*, edited by Spencer Childers, London: John Murray, 1908). Samuel Leech (*Thirty Years from Home*) deserted in New York and originally wrote his book for an American audience. He may well have been more of a British patriot in his youth than he was later

prepared to admit. He has the most acute mind and the best style of all these writers. I have quoted him more than anybody else. William Spavens (*The Narrative of W. Spavens, Chatham Pensioner, written by himself, Louth:* 1796) provides a view from an earlier and more brutal period. There is also M.O. Hay (ed.), *Landsman Hay. The Memoirs of Robert Hay, 1789–1847*, London: Rupert Hart-Davis, 1953. This concerns Hay's ancestor who ran away to sea, eventually deserted and grew up to be a journalist and write a memoir for his family in Scotland. *The Life and Surprising Adventures of Mary Anne Talbot, in the name of John Taylor . . . Related by Herself*, London: R.S. Kirby, 1806, is a fascinating book, both comic and tragic, but thin on her life as a seaman. She, too, hated and feared the press gang. John Wetherell's memoirs deal mainly with his time as a prisoner-of-war, but are notable for his bitter picture of naval discipline: C.S. Forester (ed.), *The Adventures of John Wetherell*, London: Michael Joseph, 1954. Watson's diary can be found in H.G. Thursfield (ed.), *Five Naval Journals, 1789-1817*, London: Publications of the Navy Records Society no. 91, 1951. Watson was eventually promoted to midshipman. John Nicol, on the other hand, ended his life as a lonely beggar in Edinburgh. His memoirs were taken down by a local bookseller. They provide a haunting view of the life of an uneducated and apolitical old tar: *The Life and Adventures of John Nicol, Mariner*, London: Cassell, 1937 (1st edn 1822).

Some of these memoirs have been reprinted since the first editions. In the bibliography I give all editions I have been able to find. Between them, these books provide a range of viewpoints such as we have for no other group of workers, except soldiers. Some of the men wrote for their families (Hay), some for publication (Nastyface), and some told their stories to others (Nicol). They were unusual men and they told their stories long after the events described. They mostly had axes to grind, particularly about flogging. Because they were unusual and often angry, they were also insightful. I have tended to rely more heavily on those who hated officers. The opposite loyalty is more common among naval historians, and can be found in Christopher Lloyd's evaluation of the memoirs in his *The British Seaman, 1200-1860, A Social Survey*, London: Paladin, 1970, pp.199-207.

8.  Durand, *An Able Seaman*, p.67; Leech, *Thirty Years from Home*, p.14.
9.  Nicol, *Life and Adventures*, p.39
10.  Nastyface, *Nautical Economy*, pp.2–3.
11.  This is based on Jackson's court martial, in Adm. I:5335.
12.  Lieutenant Thomas Hodgskin, *An Essay on Naval Discipline, Shewing Part of its Evil Effects*, London: Sherwood, Neely & Jones, 1813, pp.97–8.
13.  Richardson, *A Mariner of England*, p.114.
14.  William Johnson Neale, *An Account of the Mutiny at Spithead and the Nore*, London: Thomas Tegg, 1842, p.3.
15.  Leech, *Thirty Years from Home*, pp.15–16.
16.  Bechervaise, *Seafaring Life*, pp.110–11; Nastyface, *Nautical Economy*, p.6.
17.  Richardson, *A Mariner of England*, p.
18.  Quoted in J.R. Hutchinson, *The Press Gang Afloat and Ashore*, London: Eveleigh Nash, 1913, p.63.
19.  Nastyface, *Nautical Economy*, pp.x–xi.

## 2. 'If there were no punishment for selling their clothes, the men would soon be naked'

1.  Lieutenant Thomas Hodgskin, *An Essay on Naval Discipline, Shewing Part of its Evil Effects*, London: Sherwood, Neely & Jones, 1813, pp.62–3.
2.  Jack Nastyface, *Nautical Economy, or Forecastle Recollections*, Cheapside: William Robinson, 1836, pp.27–8.
3.  James Durand, *An Able Seaman of 1812*, edited by George

S. Brooks, New Haven: Yale University Press, 1926, p.18; Hodgskin, *Naval Discipline*, p.69.

4. An Officer of Rank (William Glascock), *Naval Sketch-Book*, 2 volumes, London: printed for the author, 1826, volume 1, pp.243–4.

5. Samuel Leech, *Thirty Years from Home, or a Voice from the Main Deck*, London: John Neale, 1844, pp.18–19.

6. Court martial of 12 September 1803, in Adm. I:5363. For a similar case see the court martial of Joseph Steel of the *Ville de Paris* in 1806, in Adm. I:5375.

7. Court martial of Joseph Hawkes, in Adm. I:3360.

8. Court martial of Beech and Collier, in Adm. I:5333.

9. Glascock, *Naval Sketch-Book*, volume 1, pp.245–6.

10. Ibid. pp.250–1.S

11. Dudley Pope, *The Black Ship*, London: Weidenfeld & Nicolson, 1963, p.62. I do not know whom Pope is quoting.

12. Samuel Billings of the *Excellent*, for instance, got 63 lashes for 'cheering on the lower deck' on 4 January 1803. See the ship's log, in Adm. 52:2992. Several men on the *Hermione* got 72 lashes before Pigot took over. See Dudley Pope, *Life in Nelson's Navy*, London: George Allen & Unwin, 1981, p.226.

13. Pope, *The Black Ship*, pp.332–3.

14. I have not read this explanation of the danger of flogging in any contemporary source. But it stands to reason. It also explains why some men survived 200 lashes and others died after 24. And it explains why they died after an interval following the beatings.

15. Captain Frederick Chamier, *Ben Brace, the Last of Nelson's Agamemnons*, London: R. Bentley, 1836, quoted in C. Northcote Parkinson, *Portsmouth Point, the Navy in Fiction, 1793–1815*, London: Liverpool University Press, 1948, p.62; Glascock, *Naval Sketch-Book*, volume 2.

16. Samuel Leech, *Thirty Years from Home*, p.?

17. The relevant logs of the *Culloden* are in Adm. 51:202 and Adm. 51:1130.

18. Captain Marryat, *Suggestions for the Abolition of Impressment in the Naval Service*, London: J.M. Richardson, 1822, pp.18–19. To be fair, Marryat regarded flogging men for selling their clothes as a regrettable necessity when dealing with pressed men. But he felt it was barbaric, and that if his suggested reforms were adopted this punishment could be dispensed with.

19. Hodgskin, *Naval Discipline*, pp.42–3.

20. Ibid., p.56. For the connection between grog, rage and punishment see James Peck, *Nelson's Blood – the Story of Naval Rum*, Havant: Kenneth Mason, 1982, pp.60–63. The court martial records are full of cases of drunken and insolent sailors.

21. Nastyface, *Nautical Economy*, pp.70–71.

22. Leech, *Thirty Years from Home*, p.21.

23. Nastyface, *Nautical Economy*, pp.108–9.

24. Leech, *Thirty Years from Home*, p.23. Characteristically, Leech here gives credit to an American officer. But he was also loyal to the kind memory of Lieutenant Scott of the *Macedonian*.

25. Hodgskin, *Naval Discipline*, pp.33–4.

26. Nastyface, *Nautical Economy*, pp.120–21; letter from Captain Thomas Troubridge to Admiralty, 2 January 1795, in Adm. 1:2596, Letter 133; Marryat, *Impressment*, pp.5–6.

27. Nastyface, *Nautical Economy*, pp.110–12.

28. See the introduction by Oliver Warner to William Robinson, *Jack Nastyface: Memoirs of a Seaman*, London: Wayland Publishers, 1973, p.9.


## 3. 'I have an old mother who has not seen me for eight years'

1. There are exceptions. They all happen when the ship is already in revolt and the people are negotiating with the captain. The mutineers at Spithead in 1797, for instance, were

safe enough and proud enough for their delegates to sign their letters.

2. For parallels on shore, see E.P. Thompson, 'The Crime of Anonymity' and Douglas Hay, 'Property, Authority and the Criminal Law', both in D. Hay, P. Linebaugh and E.P. Thompson (eds), *Albion's Fatal Tree, Crime and Society in Eighteenth Century England*, London: Allen Lane, 1975.

3. This account is based on the courts martial of the *Bellerephon* mutineers, in Adm. 1:5333.

4. In civilian life Cook had been an attorney practising in Lancaster. He may not have been used to working-class conventions of solidarity.

5. The petitions sent to the Admiralty are collected in Adm. I:5125. The great majority of petitions were sent to line officers and have vanished.

6. This is based on McDonough's court martial, in Adm. I:5336.

7. After reading around in the court martial transcripts from 1798 to 1815, I have the definite impression that the Admiralty and admirals became far more interested in responding to letters and investigating complaints. This was part and parcel of a general change in discipline, which I think was the result of the fear induced in officers by the frequent mutinies. I hope to take this up in a later publication.

8. William Richardson, *A Mariner of England*, edited by Spencer Childers, London: John Murray, 1908, pp.105–6

9. Ibid., pp.117–18.

10. Samuel Leech, *Thirty Years from Home, or a Voice from the Main Deck*, London: John Neale, 1844, pp.81–2.

11. The following section is based on the court martial of the Excellents, in Adm. I:5362, and the ship's log, in Adm. 52:2992.

12. Richardson (*A Mariner of England*, pp.188–9) says the *Excellent* came out to the West Indies to put down the Haitian revolt; on pp.183–95 he gives a fascinating picture of the

tensions in the West Indies at this time from the sailor's point of view. Richardson had worked on a slaver himself and was sensitive to the danger and importance of slave revolts.

## 4. 'The footballs and shuttlecocks of a set of tyrants'

1. Cockburn is quoted in Kenneth J. Logue, *Popular Disturbances in Scotland, 1780–1815*, Edinburgh: John Donald, 1979, p.133. The lines from Wordsworth come from the poem 'French Revolution, as it appeared to Enthusiasts at its Commencement'.
2. E.P. Thompson, *The Making of the English Working Class*, London: Penguin, 1968 (2nd edn), p.117.
3. C.L.R. James, *The Black Jacobins*, London: Allison & Busby, 1980 reprint, p.67.
4. Ibid.; Michael Craton, *Testing the Chains: Resistance to Slavery in the British West Indies*, Ithaca: Cornell university Press, 1982; Eugene Genovese, *From Rebellion to Revolution: Afro-American Slave Revolts in the Making of the Modern World*, New Orleans: Louisiana State U.P., 1980. Craton's book is fascinating, but for analysis I lean on James and Genovese.
5. For Europe, see R.R. Palmer, *The Age of the Democratic Revolution: A Political History of Europe and America, 1760–1800*, Princeton: Princeton University Press, 1970, volume 2.
6. Marianne Elliott, *Partners in Revolution: the United Irishmen and France*. New Haven: Yale University Press, 1982.
7. Logue, *Disturbances in Scotland*, pp.133–47.
8. Thompson, *The Making of the English Working Class*, pp.20–21 and 157–8.
9. Samuel Leech, *Thirty Years from Home, or a Voice from the Main Deck*, London: John Neale, 1843.
10. William Richardson, *A Mariner of England*, edited by Spencer Childers, London: John Murray, 1908, p.129.

11. James Dugan, *The Great Mutiny*, London: Andre Deutsch, 1966, p.278.

12. R.B. Rose, 'A Liverpool Sailor's Strike in the Eighteenth Century', *Transactions of the Lancashire and Cheshire Antiquarian Society*, 1958, volume 68, p.88.

13. Ibid., p.89.

14. This is how I read Rose's evidence on p.91. Rose himself feels it was a defeat for the strikers.

15. For an introduction to the literature on this, see Walter J. Shelton, *English Hunger and Industrial Disorders. A Study of Social Conflict during the First Decades of George III's Reign*, London: Macmillan, 1973; John Stevenson, *Popular Disturbances in England, 1700–1870*, London: Longman, 1970, pp.113–80; John Rule, *The Experience of Labour in Eighteenth-century Industry*, London: Croom Helm, 1981.

16. R.B. Rose, 'A Liverpool Sailor's Strike', p.92; Walter J. Shelton, *English Hunger*, pp.164–84.

17. Eric Hobsbawm, *Labouring Men*, London: Weidenfeld & Nicolson, 1968, p.7.

18. Thompson, *The Making of the English Working Class*, p.112.

19. See N. McCord and D.E. Brewster, 'Some Labour Troubles of the 1790s in North-east England', *International Review of Social History*, 1968, volume 12, pp.366–78. They see the officers on the spot as moderate and sensible men; I see them as scared.

20. Logue, *Disturbances in Scotland*, pp.148–53 and 160–61.

21. A. Geddes, 'Portsmouth during the great French Wars, 1770–1800', *Portsmouth Papers*, 1970, no.91, p.5.

22. A.T. Mahan, *The Influence of Sea Power upon the French Revolution and Empire, 1793–1812*, 2 volumes, London: Sampson & Low, 1892, pp.35–79.

23. Mary Anne Talbot, *The Life and Surprising Adventures of Mary Anne Talbot . . . Related by Herself*, London: R.S. Kirby, 1806.

## 5. 'I will blow them to the bounds of buggery before we come up without honourable terms'

The main source for this chapter and the next is the court martial of the *Culloden* mutineers, in Adm. I:5331. All quotations not credited to another source are taken from this transcript.

1. Ludovic Kennedy, *Nelson and his Captains*, London: Collins, 1975 (2nd edn), p.75; 'Sir Thomas Troubridge', *Dictionary of National Biography*, volume 19, Oxford: Oxford U.P. pp.1183–4; John Marshall, *Royal Naval Biography*, *Supplement*, part 1, 1827, p.279.
2. Kennedy, *Nelson and his Captains*, p.76.
3. Court martial of Troubridge and his officers for the loss of the *Castor*, in Adm. I:5331.
4. For the accident see the ship's log for 19–23 November, in Adm. 51:1130, and a letter from Captain Mann of the *Zealous* to the Admiralty on 22 November 1794, in Adm. I:2128, Letter 76.
5. Letter from Troubridge to Admiral Parker, 26 November 1794, enclosure, in Adm. I:1008, Letter 509.
6. Letter from Admiral Parker's superior, Admiral Howe, to Admiralty, 21 November 1794, in Adm. I:101, Letter 506.
7. Troubridge to Admiralty, 23 November 1794 and 26 November 1794, in Adm. I:2595, Letters 73 and 74.
8. Log of the *Culloden* for 1793, in Adm. 51:202, gives the details on deaths. The sick list is an enclosure in a letter from Admiral Gardner to Admiralty, 2 October 1793, in Adm. I:316. It is the only sick list I have ever come across: Gardner must have thought it was particularly bad. The implication is that the Cullodens were lucky to suffer so few deaths.
9. Dudley Pope, *Life in Nelson's Navy*, London: George Allen & Unwin, 1981, p.131. See also Michael A. Lewis, *A Social History of the Navy, 1793–1815*, London: George Allen & Unwin, 1960, pp.361–89 and 420.

10.  Jack Nastyface, *Nautical Economy, or Forecastle Recollections*, Cheapside: William Robinson, 1836, pp.16 and 36.

11.  William Henry Dillon, *A Narrative of my Professional Adventures*, edited by M.A. Lewis, London: Publications of the Navy Records Society 1953, no.93, volume 1, p.138.

12.  Samuel Leech, *Thirty Years from Home, or a Voice from the Main Deck*, London: John Neale, 1844, p.46.

13.  On land, too, the overwhelming majority of deaths in the army came outside battle. The Russian winter and the Caribbean mosquito were the real killers. War in this period appears to have entered a lull between the old horror that culminated in the Thirty Years War and the new horror that began with the American Civil War. This was because artillery had begun to replace hand-to-hand fighting, but the repeating rifle had not yet been invented.

14.  William Richardson, *A Mariner of England*, edited by Spencer Childers, London: John Murray, 1908, p.195.

15.  *The Life and Adventures of John Nicol, Mariner*, London: Cassell, 1937 (1st edn 1822), pp.50–51.

16.  The quote from Nelson is in A.T. Mahan, *The Influence of Sea Power upon the French Revolution and Empire, 1793– 1812*, London: Sampson, Low & Co., 1892, volume 1, p.75. The evidence on the sea-worthiness of the *Culloden* is enormous and not entirely consistent. Gardner to Admiralty, 2 October 1793, in Adm. I:316, includes a review of the state of the *Culloden* on return from the West Indies by the ship's carpenter, Dikes. Another report by Dikes some months later is included in Captain Rich to Admiralty, 1 March 1794, in Adm. I:2331. Dikes found a lot of defects, particularly problems sailing to windward and a weakness of the knees of the masts. The year after the mutiny the ship did lose the mainmast in a storm: Admiral Hotham to Admiralty, 26 November 1795, Adm. 1:393. For the state of the ship in 1797, see the mixed reports in letters from Admiral Jervis in

the Mediterranean, in Adm. 1: 396, Letters 21, 107, 141 and 244. The ship's logs for 1793 and 1794 are in Adm. 52:2867, Adm. 51:202, Adm. 51:1130 and Adm. 51:1150. These contain running accounts of repairs. Also suggestive are the large number of shipwrights and kindred trades carried on the ship's muster books for victuals only at intervals over these two years. See Adm. 36:12166–12169.

17.  Ship's log, 27 November 1794, in Adm. 51:1130.

18.  All the data in this chapter and the next about men's ages, birthplaces and ranks are taken from the ship's muster books. The relevant volume for the mutiny is Adm. 36:12169. This needs to be checked with earlier volumes since men often entered at one rank and were later promoted to another. The earlier volumes are Adm. 36:12166–12168. The data on ages are approximate. Men may have been unclear about their ages, and the clerk carried a man's age forward from one muster book to the next, so that a man's age never changed on a ship.The only exception was when he moved from 'Boy First Class' to 'Man' and his age changed from 16 to 18. For the *Culloden* I have generally added a year to each man's age to give his age at the time of the mutiny.

Many men joined the Navy under assumed names, and they may well have lied about their homes. In any case, the muster books give a man's place of birth rather than his place of residence. Sailors moved around a lot. A man born in Kerry but living in London for the last 20 years appears as Irish. A second-generation Irishman in Liverpool appears as English. This does not necessarily reflect what men thought they were. Again, a man's rank on entering the Navy does not necessarily reflect his experience of the sea. Men rated themselves, and able seamen may well have rated themselves as ordinary seamen. Writing of the American Navy in 1841, Dana said, 'There is a large proportion of ordinary seamen in the navy. This is probably because the power of the officers is so great upon their long cruises to detect and punish any deficiency, and

because, if a man can by any means be made to appear wanting in capacity for the duty he has shipped to perform, it will justify a great deal of hard usage. Men, therefore, prefer rather to underrate than to run any risk of overrating themselves.'
(Richard Henry Dana, Junior, *The Seaman's Manual*, London: Edward Moxon, 1841, p.174.) The American Navy was modelled very closely on the British, but officers were harsher in 1794 than in 1841. And there is a lot of evidence that at this period work discipline bore particularly harshly on the skilled topmen. So we must assume that many 'ordinary' seamen were in reality quite able.

19. I am quoting from a paper someone wrote for Hyman in his defence. It is possible that the words used at the time were slightly more pithy.

20. Adm. 36:12169 gives his age as 46 and Adm. 36:12167 gives his age at entry as 26. Probably the clerk miscopied.

21. John Rule, *The Experience of Labour in Eighteenth-century Industry*, London: Croom Helm, 1981, pp.152–7.

22. Admiral Parker to Admiralty, 5 December 1794, Adm.1:1008, Letter 541.

23. The following section is based on the court martial of Captain Shield and Lieutenant McKinley of the *Windsor Castle*, in Adm. I:5331. The letter from the men is an appendix to the transcript of the trial.

24. Ship's log, 11 November 1794, in Adm. 52:2537.

25. Ibid.

26. Ibid., 12 November.

27. Admiral Parker to Admiralty, 7 December 1794, in Adm. I:1008, Letter 551.

28. Report from Seymour and Pakenham enclosed, in Adm. I:1008, Letter 551.

29. Parker to Admiralty, 9 December 1794, in Adm. I:1008, Letter 556.

30. Ibid.

31. See chapters 8 and 9 and the epilogue to this book.

32. James Dugan, *The Great Mutiny*, London: Andre Deutsch, 1966, pp.108–9.

33. It should be in Adm. I:1008, Letter 557.

## 6 'The most active ringleaders and the most proper objects for a Court Martial'

The main source for this chapter is the court martial of the *Culloden* mutineers, in Adm. 1:5331. The data on ages, ranks and birthplaces are taken from the ship's muster books, Adm. 36:12166–12169.

1. Troubridge to Admiralty, 9 December 1794, in Adm. 1:2595, Letter 76.

2. Troubridge to Parker, 6 December 1794, enclosed in Parker to Admiralty, Adm. 1:1008, Letter 541.

3. Troubridge to Admiralty, 9 December 1794, Adm. I:2595, Letter 76. These must be the same as the 30 men recorded in the muster book as transferred on 29 December. After each name is written 'per pro adm order'. See Adm. 36:12169.

4. Troubridge was the prosecutor at the court martial of the *Culloden* mutineers. He was not a stupid man. The evidence against some of the ten defendants was quite thin. If Troubridge had had solid evidence against some of the 30 hard core, he would probably have tried them instead.

5. By the time of the mutiny several had been promoted. There were then eight men rated landsmen, twelve ordinary seamen, eight able seamen and a quarter gunner.

6. Troubridge to Admiralty, 18 December 1795, in Adm. I:2596, Letter 140.

7. Christian's uncle the politician changed his name from Christian to Curwen upon hearing the shameful news of the mutiny. He later served as a cabinet minister. Christian's lawyer brother led a campaign to blacken Bligh's name which was, and is, successful.

8. The sailors were quite clear on this point. See Lieutenant Thomas Hodgskin, *An Essay on Naval Discipline, Shewing Part of its Evil Effects*, London: Sherwood, Neely & Jones, 1813, p.136; Samuel Leech, *Thirty Years From Home, or a Voice from the Main Deck*, London: John Neale, 1844.

9. The official rules for courts martial were set out in John MacArthur, *A Treatise of the Principles and Practice of Naval Courts-Martial*. The first edition was published in London in 1792. The first book of its kind, it filled a felt need for court martial judges. It went through many editions during the war years. It does not conform strictly to the rules on shore. More important, there are many things it tells officers not to do. By implication, they were doing these things.

10. Court martial of the *Excellent* mutineers, in Adm. 1:5362.

11. Court martial of 31 January, in Adm. 1:5363; court martial of 15–16 October 1803, in Adm. 1:5364; court martial of 27 June 1808, in Adm. 1:5387. As the war ground on there was an increasing tendency to try men under specific articles of war. This was probably the result of the increasing influence of MacArthur, *Principles and Practice of Naval Courts-Martial*. MacArthur was very firm about specifying the article of war.

12. Court martial of the *Defiance* mutineers, in Adm. I:5334.

13. Leech, *Thirty Years from Home*, pp.31–32.

14. To testify, Pakenham had to leave his seat as a judge, move across and take the oath, testify, and then return to his seat as a judge. The admiral of the fleet was not allowed to sit at a court martial. This was to protect his subordinates. But it was common practice for officers deeply involved in putting down a mutiny to sit as judges.

15. This may, or may not, have been true. Certainly Hyman's evidence about the master has the ring of an authentic grudge. But it is probable that after being slapped he got off his hammock and joined the mutineers.

16. Whitter testified very little at the trial. Probably Troubridge did not want anybody asking him embarrassing questions.

17. Troubridge to Admiralty, 9 December 1794, in Adm. 1:2595, Letter 76.

18. Justice worked the same way on shore. See Douglas Hay, 'Property, Authority and the Criminal Law', in D. Hay, P. Linebaugh and E.P. Thompson (eds), *Albion's Fatal Tree, Crime and Society in Eighteenth Century England*, London: Allen Lane, 1975. The same method is still used in political trials all over the world to this day.

19. Leech, *Thirty Years from Home*, p.32

20. For the *Hermione*, see the prologue to this book.

21. For the *Marlborough*, see Ludovic Kennedy, *Nelson and his Captains*, London: Collins, 1975 (2nd edn), pp.84–5.

22. John Nicol, *The Life and Adventures of John Nicol, Mariner*, London: Cassell, 1937 (1st edn 1822), pp.59–60.

23. As on shore. See Hay, 'Property, Authority and the Criminal Law'.

24. Court martial of the *Excellent* mutineers, in Adm. I:5362.

25. The ship's muster book, in Adm. 36:12169, and the ship's log, in Adm. 51:1130.

26. The ship's log, in ibid.

27. Captain Rich's log, in Adm. 51:202, and Captain Troubridge's log, in Adm. 51:1130.

28. Troubridge's log for the floggings. For the men run I have used the *Culloden* muster book, in Adm. 36:12170. This includes lists of men run at the end of each series of musters, but the lists are incomplete. You have to go through the musters man by man to get an accurate count.

29. Logs of the *Culloden*, August 1794 to July 1800, in Adm. 51:1130, 1132, 1199, 1241, 1294 and 1313.

30. Admiral Hotham to Admiralty, 14 July 1795, in Adm. 1:393, Letter 191; Kennedy, *Nelson and his Captains*, p.67.

31. Kennedy, *Nelson and his Captains*, pp.84–6.

32. Enclosure in Jervis to Admiralty, 16 June 1797, in Adm. 1:396, Letter 107.

33. Kennedy, *Nelson and his Captains*, pp.129 and 188.

34. Log of the *Culloden*, in Adm. 51:1313.

35. Kennedy, *Nelson and his Captains*, pp.337–8; 'Sir Thomas Troubridge', *Dictionary of National Biography*, volume 19, pp.1183–4, Oxford: Oxford U.P.

## 7. 'My constant prayer to heaven is that my daughters may never set foot on board of a man-of-war'

1. My discussion of grog is based on James Peck, *Nelson's Blood – The Story of Naval Rum*, Havant: Kenneth Mason, 1982.

2. Workers of all kinds in the eighteenth century had a strong sense of traditional rights. Nowadays, we tend to think of prices as outside our control. We understand that we get the wages we fight for. Then, most people felt that there was a right traditional price for each commodity and a right traditional wage for each job. They often demonstrated or rioted when those prices went up or wages down. But in the 1790s workers were shifting to the idea that strikes and solidarity at work were the best way to fight. The naval mutinies of the 1790s are part of this shift. See E.P. Thompson, 'The Moral Economy of the English Crowd in the Eighteenth Century', *Past and Present*, 1971, no. 50, pp.76–136; Elizabeth Fox-Genovese, 'The Many Faces of the Moral Economy: A Contribution to a Debate', *Past and Present*, 1973, no. 58, pp.160–8; Roger Wells, 'The Revolt of the South-West, 1800–1801: A Study in English Popular Protest', *Social History*, 1977, volume 6, pp.713–44; Alan Booth, 'Food Riots in the North-west of England, 1790–1801', *Past and Present*, 1977, no. 77, pp.84–107. An outraged sense of the moral economy runs right through the attack on Bligh by Morrison, one of the *Bounty* mutineers. See Owen Rutter (ed.), *The Journal of James Morrison*, London: Golden Cockrel Press, 1935, especially pp.18ff.

3. Lieutenant Thomas Hodgskin, *An Essay on Naval*

*Discipline, Shewing Part of its Evil Effects*, London: Sherwood, Neely & Jones, 1813, pp.97–8.

4. For the *Hermione* see the prologue to this book. For the connection between grog and punishment see Peck, *Nelson's Blood*, pp.57–63.

5. Samuel Leech, *Thirty Years from Home, or a Voice from the Main Deck*, Boston: Tappan & Dennet, p.65.

6. John Nicol, *The Life and Adventures of John Nicol, Mariner*, London: Cassell, 1937 (1st edn 1822), p.193.

7. For an introduction to homosexuality in the Navy see Arthur N. Gilbert, 'Sexual Deviance and Disaster during the Napoleonic Wars', *Albion*, 1977, volume 9, pp.98–113.

8. Jack Nastyface, *Nautical Economy, or Forecastle Recollections*, Cheapside: William Robinson, 1836, pp.59–61.

9. Leech, *Thirty Years from Home*, p.114; William Richardson, *A Mariner of England*, edited by Spencer Childers, London: John Murray, 1908, p.226.

10. An Officer of Rank (William Glascock), *Naval Sketch-Book*, London: printed for the author, volume 1, pp.202–5.

11. Nastyface, *Nautical Economy*, pp.63–8.

12. Leech, p.66.

13. Ibid., p.26.

## 8. 'Liberty and no more five-water grog!

This chapter is largely based on the court martial of the *Defiance* mutineers, in Adm. 1:5334. The data on age, place of birth and rating on board come from the ship's muster books for 1795–6, in Adm. 36:11909–11910.

1. Captain Home to Admiralty, 3 January 1796, in Adm. 1:1915, Letter 311.

2. The high proportion of quota men can be seen from the muster books. By and large the quota area is different from the place of birth.

3. Home to Duncan, enclosed in Duncan to Admiralty, 27 July 1795, in Adm. 1:522, Letter 137; Duncan to Admiralty, no date, in Adm. 1:522, Letter 143.

4. In Buckinghamshire Richard North was given the choice of the army or Navy for getting Elizabeth Foulkes with child. In 1795 a bricklayer's apprentice got the same sentence for stealing a scaffold board. For these and other examples see Clive Elmsley, 'The Recruitment of Petty Offenders during the French Wars, 1793–1815', *Mariners' Mirror*, 1980, volume 66, pp.199–208.

5. Home to Duncan, enclosed in Duncan to Admiralty, 27 July 1795, in Adm. 1:522, Letter 137.

6. Ibid.

7. The best analysis of this process is in Gavin Kennedy, *Bligh*, London: Duckworth, 1978, pp.17–112.

8. Ludovic Kennedy, *Nelson and his Captains*, London: Collins, 1975, p.131.

9. The letter is attached to the court martial record. I say Graham 'probably' wrote it: he certainly wrote the later letter from the ship's company, printed in the next chapter.

## 9. 'How came he to sleep in your hammock with you that night?'

This chapter, like the last, is largely based on the court martial of the *Defiance* mutineers, in Adm. I:5334. The data on age, place of birth and rating on board come from the ship's muster books for 1795–6, in Adm. 36:11909–11910.

1. Gavin Kennedy, 'Bligh and the *Defiance* Mutiny', *Mariners' Mirror*, 1979, volume 65, pp.65–8.

2. There were four separate mutinies by fencible regiments in Scotland between March 1794 and June 1795; John Prebble, *Mutiny: Highland Regiments in Revolt 1743–1804*, London: Penguin, 1975, pp.262–391. For the militia riots, start with

Roger Wells, 'The Militia Mutinies of 1795' in John Rule (ed.), *Outside the Law: Studies in Crime and Order, 1650–1850*, Exeter: University of Exeter, Exeter Papers in Economic History no. 15, 1983.

3. John Nicol, *The Life and Adventures of John Nicol, Mariner*, London: Cassell, 1937 (1st edn 1822), pp. 180–1.

4. For the situation in 1795 see John Ehrman, *The Younger Pitt*, London: Constable, 1983, volume 2, pp.441–76; Roger Wells, *Insurrection: The British Experience, 1795–1803*, Gloucester; Alan Sutton, 1983, pp.44–65.

5. This is taken from a copy of the letter, enclosed in Pringle to Admiralty, 19 October 1795, in Adm. I:522, Letter 275.

6. Kennedy, 'Bligh and the *Defiance* Mutiny'.

7. Pringle to Admiralty, 20 October 1795, in Adm. 1:522, Letter 278.

8. Pringle to Admiralty, 21 October 1795 and 23 October 1795, in Adm. 1:522, Letters 280 and 283.

9. Log of the *Defiance* for 6 March, in Adm. 51:1101.

10. Letter from Bligh to the admiral at the Nore, 14 January 1796, in Adm. 1:726, Letter 56.

11. Log of the *Defiance* for 8 March, in Adm. 51:1101.

12. Log of the *Defiance* for 9 March; the muster books for 1796, in Adm. 36:11910.

13. Court martial of the *Terrible* mutineers, in Adm. 1:5333; solicitors to Admiralty, 14 March 1796, in Adm. 1:3684; Admiral Hotham to Admiralty, 12 September 1795, 21 September 1795 and 10 October 1795, in Adm. 1:393, Letters 225, 228 and 242.


## Epilogue 'A red flag at the mizzen topmast head'

This account of the Spithead mutiny follows James Dugan, *The Great Mutiny*, London: Andre Deutsch, 1966; Conrad Gill, *The Naval Mutinies of 1797*, Manchester: Manchester University Press, 1913; Roger Wells, *Insurrection: The British*

*Experience, 1795–1803*, Gloucester: Alan Sutton, 1983. Wells is particularly good on the role of the United Irishmen.

1. Dugan, *The Great Mutiny*, London: Andre Deutsch, 1966, p.278.
2. Muster books of the *Royal George* for 1793, in Adm. 36:11699, for 1797, in Adm. 36:11704.
3. Muster books for the *Defiance*, in Adm. 36:11909–11910; muster book for the *Director*, in Adm. 36:12781.

# Sources

Most of this book is based on the records of courts-martial. At each trial a clerk took down a complete verbatim record of everything said. This record was then sent to the Admiralty in London. The Admiralty had to decide on appeals for clemency, and they needed the complete records to make up their minds. These court-martial records for our period are now all in the Public Record Office in Kew, London.

They are an extraordinarily rich source for historians. Normally historians of the struggles of the eighteenth-century working class have to work largely from spies' reports and brief summaries of trials. In the naval records it is possible to hear the sailors speaking. But there are problems with the court-martial records.

The major problem is that they provide a record of *defeated* protests. The mutiny on the *Windsor Castle* in 1795 was more important than the mutiny on the *Culloden* the next month. But the Windsor Castles won their demand that nobody be victimized afterwards. So this book devotes far more space to the Cullodens than the Windsor Castles.

Moreover, at the court martial the prosecutor was by custom the captain of the unruly ship. The defendants were his seamen. The witnesses were mostly his officers and petty officers. Again and again, the court records show the prosecutor trying to establish that the men gave no warning of their feelings and made no prior protest. If they had protested through 'normal' channels and gained no redress, this might mitigate their offense. It would also reflect badly on the captain who had been neither firm enough to suppress unrest nor fair enough to defuse it. The court, of course, was composed of the prosecutor's fellow captains and perhaps an admiral. The prosecutor did not want his incompetence exposed in front of them.

So seamen and officers were discouraged from mentioning earlier protests. On the *Terrible*, for instance, her particularly unpleasant captain had faced several deputations complaining about bad bread before the men mutinied over the issue (see Adm. I:5333). During the trial he was at some pains to establish that the men had not protested, and that when they had done so they had been given satisfaction.

Defendants also usually had more sense than to anger the court by trying to justify their actions. All this means that you sometimes have to read 30 or 40 pages of a court-martial before discovering what a mutiny was about. Sometimes the reader never finds out.

But of course the court was composed of human beings. They were curious, and they could not actually judge the case without knowing the background. Usually they knew already. But often the record contains enlightening questions from the court, presumably put by a captain who cannot figure out what is going on, or wants to confirm a rumour he has heard.

It is possible to combine such accidental illuminations with other evidence to glean some idea of organisation below decks. But the bias in the records means that we see only the tip of the iceberg. The protests we know most about were more violent and less successful than the average run of protests.

There is a general tendency for collective protests to disappear from other records. A captain who dealt with the matter without a court-martial would be unlikely to mention it in an official letter. Nor would the master usually make any note of it in the ship's log. Even where a mutiny ended in court martial, historians have tended to forget it. The entry on Troubridge in the *The Dictionary of National Biography*, for instance, misses out the *Culloden* mutiny completely. The wave of strikes in 1797 involved tens of thousands of men and won several demands, most notably the replacement of over a hundred officers at Spithead and a substantial pay rise for all sailors. It was the most successful large strike of its time. The general strike of 1842 was bigger, but went down to defeat. There was no successful strike on the same scale until the dock strike of 1889. But naval historians have, for understandable reasons, tended to skirt this episode. The historians who have treated the strikes have almost all paid more attention to the defeat at the Nore than to the victory at Spithead. Spithead was more important, but there were no courts martial afterwards and so the records are much thinner.

In short, every source tends to conceal successful collective actions. There is another problem with court-martial records. Most seamen on most ships stayed resolutely silent. A few petty officers testified. Their evidence often served to hang a man, but they were usually not verbose witnesses. Officers were much the best prosecution witnesses. They shared the values and loyalties of the court, so they were more likely to be believed. They were more at ease, and therefore more lucid and fluent. Lower deck activists quite rightly lied themselves blue in the face to save their heads and their mates. So we have to rely largely on officers' accounts of what happened. They are more detailed and more truthful. But besides the obvious bias, they had no concrete idea of how the men organized. This was because organization was the thing the people were concealing. So the officers' testimony usually concentrates on overt acts: one seaman was standing sentry with a pike or another battered down the ward room door.

In any case, the court wanted all witnesses to concentrate on overt acts. The court was trying to be fair, and to be seen to be fair. They therefore did not go into the question of whether the captain of the people were in the right. After all, the people were so often in the right. Instead, the court concerned itself with the simpler matter of whether such individual prisoner had committed specific overt acts. The result was that an angry sailor who had been rude to an officer could be hanged as easily as the organizer of a mutiny.

# Bibliography

This bibliography includes only books and articles referred to in the notes. However, three recent books contain excellent bibliographies. All three are included below. Dudley Pope, *Life in Nelson's Navy*, is a work of great scholarship and easy reading by the naval novelist. The bibliography includes all the books you should read and leaves out all the books you should not read: an amazing feat. Marianne Elliott, *Partners in Revolution: The United Irishmen and France*, has changed our whole understanding of Ireland in 1798. The bibliography covers much more than that. Roger Wells, *Insurrection: The British Experience, 1795–1803*, is a work of terrifying scholarship and rollicking revolutionary enthusiasm. It is a difficult book for the beginner (skip chapter 2). But it provides a startling picture of a mass movement of working-class revolutionaries. It is very good on the naval mutinies of 1797, and the bibliography is comprehensive.

## Unpublished sources

All the letters and records referred to in the notes can be found in the Admiralty records. These are kept in the Public Records Office in Ruskin Avenue, Kew, London. These records are *public*: they can be read by anybody, and anybody can get a reader's ticket. The staff are very helpful in explaining how to find the documents you want.

Published sources

John Bechervaise, *Thirty-Six Years of a Seafaring Life*, Portsea: 1839.

Alan Booth, 'Food Riots in the North-west of England 1790–1801', *Past and Present*, 1977, no. 77, pp.84–107.

Michael Craton, *Breaking the Chains: Resistance to Slavery in the British West Indies*, Ithaca: Cornell University Press, 1982.

Richard Henry Dana, Junior, *The Seaman's Manual*, London: Edward Moxon, 1841.

William Henry Dillon, *A Narrative of my Professional Adventures*, edited by M.A. Lewis, London: Publications of the Navy Records Society. no. 93, 1953

James Dugan, *The Great Mutiny*, London: Andre Deutsch, 1966.

James Durand, *An Able Seaman of 1812*, edited by George S. Brooks, New Haven: Yale University Press, 1926.

John Ehrman, *The Younger Pitt*, volume 2, London: Constable, 1983.

Marianne Elliott, *Partners in Revolution: The United Irishmen and France*, New Haven: Yale University Press, 1982.

Clive Elmsley, 'The Recruitment of Petty Offenders during the French Wars, 1793–1815', *Mariners' Mirror*, 1980, volume 66, pp.199–208.

C.S. Forester, (ed.), *The Adventures of John Wetherell*, London: Michael Joseph, 1954.

Elizabeth Fox-Genovese, 'The Many Faces of the Moral Economy: A Contribution to a Debate', *Past and Present*, 1973, no. 58, pp.160–8.

A. Geddes, 'Portsmouth during the Great French Wars, 1770–1800', *Portsmouth Papers*, 1970, no. 9.

Eugene Genovese, *From Rebellion to Revolution: Afro-American Slave Revolts in the Making of the Modern World* New Orleans: Louisiana State U.P. 1980.

Arthur N. Gilbert, 'Sexual Deviance and Disaster during the

Napoleonic Wars', *Albion*, 1977, volume 9, pp.98–113.

Conrad Gill, *The Naval Mutinies of 1797*, Manchester: Manchester University Press, 1913.

William Glascock (An Officer of Rank), *Naval Sketch-Book*, 2 volumes, London: printed for the author, 1826.

Douglas Hay, 'Property, Authority and the Criminal Law', in D. Hay, P. Linebaugh and E.P. Thompson (eds), *Albion's Fatal Tree, Crime and Society in Eighteenth Century England*, London: Allen Lane, 1975.

M.D. Hay (ed.), *Landsman Hay. The Memoirs of Robert Hay, 1789–1847*, London: Rupert Hart-Davis, 1953.

Eric Hobsbawm, *Labouring Men*, London: Weidenfeld & Nicolson, 1968.

Thomas Hodgskin, *An Essay on Naval Discipline, Shewing Part of its Evil Effects*, London: Sherwood, Neely & Jones, 1813.

J.R. Hutchinson, *The Press Gang Afloat and Ashore*, London: Eveleigh Nash, 1913.

C.L.R. James, *The Black Jacobins*, London: Allison & Busby, 1980 edition.

Gavin Kennedy, *Bligh*, London: Duckworth, 1978.

Gavin Kennedy, 'Bligh and the *Defiance* mutiny', *Mariners' Mirror*, 1979, volume 65, pp.65–8.

Ludovic Kennedy, *Nelson and his Captains*, London: Collins, 1975 (2nd edn).

Samuel Leech, *Thirty Years from Home, or a Voice from the Main Deck*, Boston: Tappan & Dennet, 1843. Reprinted London: John Neale, 1844 and in *The Magazine of History*, 1905, extra no. 9, New York.

Michael A. Lewis, *A Social History of the Navy, 1793–1815*, London: George Allen & Unwin, 1960.

Christopher Lloyd, *The British Seaman, 1200–1860, A Social Survey*, London: Paladin, 1970.

Kenneth J. Logue, *Popular Disturbances in Scotland*, Edinburgh: John Donald, 1979.

John MacArthur, *A Treatise of the Principles and Practice of*

*Naval Courts-Martial*, London: 1792. Republished in several revised editions.

N. McCord and D.E. Brewster, 'Some Labour Troubles of the 1790s in North-east England', *International Review of Social History*, 1968, volume 12, pp.266–78.

A.T. Mahan, *The Influence of Sea Power upon the French Revolution and Empire, 1793–1812*, 2 volumes, London: Sampson & Low, 1892.

Captain Marryat, *Suggestions for the Abolition of Impressment in the Naval Service*, London: J.M. Richardson, 1822.

John Marshall, *Royal Naval Biography, Supplement*, London: 1827.

Jack Nastyface, *Nautical Economy, or Forecastle Recollections of Events During the Last War, Dedicated to the Brave Tars of Old England, by a Sailor, Politely Called by the Officers of the Navy, Jack Nasty-Face*, London: William Robinson, 1836. Reprinted with an introduction by Oliver Warner as William Robinson, *Jack Nastyface: Memoirs of a Seaman*, London: Wayland Publishers, 1973.

Jonathan Neale, 'Mutiny and Discipline in the Royal Navy, 1793–1815', MA thesis, University of Warwick, 1984.

William Johnson Neale, *An Account of the Mutiny at Spithead and the Nore*, London: Thomas Tegg, 1842.

John Nicol, *The Life and Adventures of John Nicol, Mariner*, edited by John Howell, Edinburgh: W. Blackwood, 1822. Reprinted with a foreword and afterword by Alexander Laing, London: Cassell, 1937.

R.R. Palmer, *The Age of the Democratic Revolution: A Political History of Europe and America, 1760–1800*, 2 volumes, Princeton: Princeton University Press, 1969–70.

C. Northcote Parkinson, *Portsmouth Point: the Navy in Fiction, 1793–1815*, London: Liverpool University Press, 1948.

James Peck, *Nelson's Blood – The Story of Naval Rum*, Havant: Kenneth Mason, 1982.

Dudley Pope, *The Black Ship*, London: Weidenfeld & Nicolson, 1963.

Dudley Pope, *Life in Nelson's Navy*, London: George Allen & Unwin, 1981.

John Prebble, *Mutiny: Highland Regiments in Revolt, 1743–1804*, London: Penguin, 1975.

William Richardson, *A Mariner of England*, edited by Spencer Childers, London: John Murray, 1908. Reprinted London: Conway Maritime Press, 1970.

R.B. Rose, 'A Liverpool Sailors' Strike in the Eighteenth Century', *Transactions of the Lancashire and Cheshire Antiquarian Society*, 1958, volume 68, pp.84–92.

John Rule, *The Experience of Labour in Eighteenth-century Industry*, London: Croom Helm, 1981.

Owen Rutter (ed.), *The Journal of James Morrison*, London, Golden Cockrel Press, 1935.

Walter J. Shelton, *English Hunger and Industrial Disorders. A Study of Social Conflict during the First Decade of George III's Reign*, London: Macmillan, 1973.

William Spavens, *The Narrative of W. Spavens, Chatham Pensioner, written by himself*, Louth: 1796.

John Stevenson, *Popular Disturbances in England, 1700–1870*, London: Longman, 1970.

Mary Anne Talbot, *The Life and Surprising Adventures of Mary Anne Talbot, in the name of John Taylor . . . Related by Herself*, London: R.S. Kirby, 1806.

E.P. Thompson, *The Making of the English Working Class*, London: Penguin, 1968 (2nd edn).

E.P. Thompson, 'The Moral Economy of the English Crowd in the Eighteenth Century', *Past and Present*, 1971, no. 50, pp.76–136.

E.P. Thompson, 'The Crime of Anonymity' in D. Hay, P. Linebaugh and E.P. Thompson (eds), *Albion's Fatal Tree, Crime and Society in Eighteenth Century England*, London: Allen Lane, 1975.

H.G. Thursfield (ed.), *Five Naval Journals, 1789–1817*, London: Publications of the Navy Records Society no. 91, 1951.

Roger Wells, 'The Revolt of the South-west, 1800–1801: A Study in English Popular Protest', *Social History*, 1977, volume 6, pp.713–44.

Roger Wells, 'The Militia Mutinies of 1795', in John Rule (ed.), *Outside the Law: Studies in Crime and Order, 1650–1850*, Exeter: University of Exeter, Exeter Papers in Economic History no. 15, 1983.

Roger Wells, *Insurrection: The British Experience, 1795–1803*, Gloucester: Alan Sutton, 1983.

# Index